Meditations
for Adults

WALLACE
FRIDY

Meditations
for Adults

ABINGDON PRESS
New York   Nashville

MEDITATIONS FOR ADULTS

Copyright © 1965 by Abingdon Press

Library of Congress Catalog Card Number: 65-20362

Scripture quotations unless otherwise noted are
from the Revised Standard Version of the Bible,
copyrighted 1946 and 1952 by the Division of
Christian Education, National Council of Churches,
and are used by permission.

SET UP, PRINTED, AND BOUND BY THE
PARTHENON PRESS, AT NASHVILLE,
TENNESSEE, UNITED STATES OF AMERICA

To

Arthur L. Humphries
and
F. M. Roddey

Churchmen
Businessmen
Sportsmen
Friends through the years

Foreword

The late Charles P. Steinmetz said that some day people will learn that material things, of themselves, do not bring happiness and are of little use in making men and women creative and powerful. Someday, he says, scientists of the world will turn their laboratories over to the study of God and prayer and the spiritual forces which as yet have hardly been scratched.

This book is sent out with the hope that in quiet moments alone, and in company with others, those who use it may be drawn closer to that unseen world of the spirit and to him who is the source of all life.

In the quietness of worship man is trying to catch those deeper currents of life which open up the larger meaning of all our little words and deeds. When we think of the glory, majesty, and perfection of God, immediately we want to bend our knees in adoration and reverence. Contemplating his greatness and power lifts us out of ourselves and prepares us for communion with him.

7

In the presence of God we can be conscious of only one thing, our sinfulness. When we fasten our minds and hearts upon the wonder and glory of God as we see him in Jesus Christ, we cry out with Isaiah, who falls upon his face, crying, "Woe is me, for I am a man of unclean lips . . . and mine eyes have seen the King, the Lord of Hosts." Evelyn Underhill says: "In Revelation it is the saints and elders nearest God who cast down their crowns when they adore him. The lesser fry, further off, are quite content to go on wearing theirs!" Albert E. Day expresses it like this: "It is commonplace to those who have studied the lives of the saints that the beginning of the experience of conscious fellowship with God is always purgation—a newly awakened conscience, shame for what one has been and is, and a vigorous effort to do and to be better."

These meditations in their original and amplified form were sermons, wrought out of the daily experiences and needs of a pastor with his people. Now it is hoped that they will reach a much wider audience and will be used in varied ways. Not only are they prepared for private use, but it is hoped that they might be useful to those who are to lead others in worship, and that busy pastors might find here suggestions in sermon preparation. It is also hoped that small prayer groups will find here material helpful in guiding meditation.

At the close of each chapter are aids to assist the leader in conducting worship services, and the prayers included may also be helpful in private devotions.

Thus, these messages are sent out with the prayer that they may help draw all who read them in private, or who are led by them in public, closer to him who gave his life for us all—Jesus Christ, our Lord.

WALLACE FRIDY

Contents

For Special Days

1
By the Power of God

We are living today in an age of power and on every hand are confronted with power in life. In the realm of science power has come to mean something dreadful when we think of all the energy which can now be released in destruction. In international affairs the concept of military power and might has taken on new proportions.

But when we turn to our New Testament we find this word "power" also used. It is a different kind of power than is frequently referred to in today's world. Paul speaks of power in the ninth verse of the twelfth chapter of II Corinthians: "My grace is sufficient for you, for my power is made perfect in weakness."

Of course Paul is speaking here of the power of God in human life. He speaks of power being made perfect in weakness. This is a strange paradox—how through weakness we can become strong. Let us look at this paradox.

In the first place, we find this true in handicapped lives—how in weakness men have become strong. Calling the roll of the great of the past is to list the names of many who contended with physical defects. Many who have become heroes in service to their country or to humanity have done so in spite of their handicaps, and maybe because of them. The stories of men who have achieved in spite of their handicaps are thrilling ones. The struggle to overcome some handicap helped to develop capacities which otherwise would have remained dormant.

In the second place, the weakness which is ours can lead us to come to God for help. We approach God through a felt sense of need. In our weakness we feel the need for help beyond our own. The feeling of inadequacy turns us to God through prayer for help. Indeed, in weakness we are strong.

Divine power cannot help the self-sufficient man. This is why pride and self-righteousness are at the root of all sin. The proud man feels no need for God. He even turns his back upon God. He is sufficient unto himself.

James Reid puts it like this: "Self-confidence is a good quality, provided it is based not on self-sufficiency but on a deep dependence on God. We come to that dependence only when self-sufficiency has been broken by some situation or experience that is too much for us. When self in its various forms is laid in dust, God can fully come in."

The point of Paul's weakness became the place of God's power. Paul's confidence in the power he possesses does not rest on self-confidence but on his confidence and dependence upon God in Christ, and he is sure that this power of God, whose spirit lives in him, will make him strong. This is what he means by power being made perfect in weakness.

James Reid reminds us that it may be that God refuses to remove our weakness because he needs it. He cites what W. Hale White says about John Bunyan:

The Creator gets the appointed task out of his servants in many ways. It is sufficient to give some of them love, sunrises and sunsets and primrose woods in spring: others have to be scourged with bloody whips or driven nearly mad by dreams . . . before they do what God has determined for them. . . . We may say of men like Bunyan that it is not their strength taken by itself which makes them remarkable and precious, but rather the conflict of strength and weakness.

Then White tells us that our weakness can bring its compensation when he says, "When God adds he subtracts; when he subtracts he adds." Thus, through our weakness God's power can be released through us in courage, our illness can give us more sympathy for the troubles of others, our sorrow can add mellowness to life, and our failures can spur us on to achievements. Strength and weakness—tied together.

In the third place, in weakness the power of God can be released through us. This fact rests on the Cross. In the Cross we see how because of the weakness of man God's power was released and let loose in the world—we see how Christ died because of the

15

weakness he shared with all humanity. In this event he shared in the sufferings to which all humanity is subject. But through that very weakness God's power was released.

This pictures for us how when we die to self and to sin, new life can arise in us through Christ. It is like a seed sown in the earth, which dies to itself, that a new creation can come forth in life. In Paul's life this same process is at work. Through his surrender to Christ he died. The old self passed away; the new self was born. The old self was crucified on the judgment of the Cross. Paul confesses that in his own weakness the power of God in Christ overtook him and made him strong.

This tells us so much today. It tells us that self must be crucified so that God's spirit may arise within our hearts. It tells us that pride must die a death, that new power and dependence upon God can make us strong. It tells us that prejudice must go and die a little death, so that new life in Christ and love for all men may arise within our hearts. When we are crucified in weakness, then we can live by the power of God.

Paul tells us that we enter into the death and resurrection of Christ. In Romans 6:4 he writes: "We were buried therefore with him by baptism into death, so that as Christ was raised from the dead by the glory of the Father, we too might walk in newness of life." "This," as James Reid says, "is the essence of the conversion experience. It is to die because we are crucified with Christ, and through death to live because he lives in us."

Thus, "My grace is sufficient for you, for my power is made perfect in weakness."

AIDS TO WORSHIP

Hymns: "Guide Me, O Thou Great Jehovah"
            "Be Strong"
Scripture: II Cor. 12:1-10

A PRAYER

Eternal God, before whose majesty and power we bow down, and in whose love we stand upon our feet, we thank thee for this day and this hour. Gratefully we come before thee, who art ruler and designer of our universe, and yet who art concerned in the affairs of our daily life.

We lay bare before thee ourselves and our needs, our hopes and our dreams, our successes and our failures, assured that from thee we gain the power needed to confront life with victory. We set aside this hour to the end that we might find thee, and in finding thee to give ourselves anew to thy love and mercy, made known in Christ. In his name we pray. Amen.

2
From Stones to Spirit

A few years ago I stood at Jacob's well, forty miles north of Jerusalem, a well dug by Jacob in his field near Shechem. It was at Jacob's well that Jesus met the Samaritan woman and asked her for a drink of water. A church has enclosed the well since the early fifth century and is the property of the Greek Orthodox Church.

It was at this spot, referred to in the fourth chapter of John, that Jesus asked the Samaritan woman for water. He speaks to her, you remember, of living water that quenches the thirst of the spirit. Then perceiving that Jesus was a prophet who understood her past and who dared to ask a Samaritan woman for water, the Jews having no dealing with the Samaritans, she asked him about the place to worship.

She said, "Our father worshiped on this mountain, and you say that in Jerusalem is the place men ought to worship."

Here she was speaking of Mt. Gerizim which overlooks the well, and which is the holy mountain of the Samaritans. The Jews, after their return from captivity in 538 B.C., refused to consider the inhab-

itants of Samaria as Jews because they had intermarried with the Gentiles. Therefore, the Samaritans
built on Mt. Gerizim a rival temple to that of Jerusalem. The ruins of that temple still can be seen on
that mountain.

So, she was asking where it was that men ought
to worship—on this mountain revered by her fathers
or in Jerusalem. Jesus answered her by saying,

Woman, believe me, the hour is coming when neither
on this mountain nor in Jerusalem will you worship the
Father. . . . But the hour is coming, and now is, when
the true worshipers will worship the Father in spirit and
truth, for such the Father seeks to worship him. God is
spirit, and those who worship him must worship in spirit
and truth. (John 4:21-24.)

*The first impression one gets of the Holy Land is
that the place where our faith had its beginning is not
where apparently it is felt most today.* In this wonderful little Holy Land there is so much which is foreign
to the spirit of Christ, so much which is contrary to
his nature.

Historically this land has been witness to conquests
and wars, to destruction and rebuilding. This area
has served as a stage for the rise and fall of successive
civilizations. Canaanites, Egyptians, Babylonians,
Persians, Greeks, Romans, Byzantines, Arabs, Cru-
saders, and many others have been masters of this
land.

Today the Holy City itself is divided into armed

camps—Jordan on one side and Israel on the other. Jesus foresaw what was going to happen to Jerusalem and to Mt. Gerizim.

So, we must move in our faith from the realm of time to timeless truth. We must move from the stones we see marking the ancient sites of yesterday to the spirit of our faith—from stones to spirit. We must move from the place to the fact behind the place, to the truth inherent within, from the place to the person, from a world of material to one of spirit.

What a wonderful experience it is to visit the place where it all happened! But through it all you come to the conclusion that our faith is not one of location or place; it is not one of time or period; but rather it is one for all the ages. It is a spiritual faith. Just why God selected the Holy Land to make himself known at a point of time in a supreme way in the form that man can understand in the person of Jesus Christ, we do not know. But what happened here is not limited to the lands of the Middle East, nor to the first century, but is for all the world and for all time. "God is spirit, and those who worship him must worship in spirit and truth."

So, when we see the place and when we remember the time, we must move in our thinking beyond time to the timeless truths represented there.

And this means that wherever we are and whenever we live, God seeks to make his will and himself known to us, that our faith is not one which beckons *to the past but which points to the future.* It is a glorious faith that is anchored in time, at a point in history, but also one which is always contemporary. This means that God is alive and that Christ is present here with us. It means that we get our bearings through the Holy Scriptures on what God has done for us through Christ, but also we find through these same Scriptures God speaking to us today.

To be sure, it is a priceless experience to visit the lands of biblical history, and it does help to make the Bible live in a special way for those who have this opportunity, but the reality of the gospel truth is not dependent upon such a visit. Ours is a spiritual religion, and God through his Holy Spirit moves among men in every place and in every age.

So, for us all God is here today wanting to touch our hearts, seeking to give us the strength we need to face life, assuring us that we need never be afraid for he is nearer than breathing, closer than hands or feet. He is here knocking at the door. "Behold, I stand at the door, and knock; if anyone hears my voice and opens the door, I will come in to him and eat with him, and he with me." Indeed, "God is spirit, and those who worship him must worship him in spirit and truth."

AIDS TO WORSHIP

Hymns: "Faith of Our Fathers"
       "He Leadeth Me"
Scripture: John 4:1-24

A Prayer

Eternal God, once again we come into thy presence to lift our hearts in praise to thee. We know that in thee we live and move and have our being. It is thou, O God, the uncreated one, who hast created us. It is thou who dost hold within thy hand the slender thread of life.

We thank thee that thou hast given to us these days of our earthly pilgrimage and hast a place and a purpose for each of us. We are grateful to believe that thou hast called us to serve thee in faithfulness and in dedication. We do not know what each day will bring forth, but we do know him whom we have believed, and we are willing to trust each day to him. Give us a sense of thy gracious presence as we live day by day, through Jesus Christ, our Lord. Amen.

3
What Is the Good News?

We live in a world that bombards us with bad news. Every day through the various news media we are confronted with what happened yesterday, almost too frightful to contemplate, and also with what may happen tomorrow, adding to our fears.

Into this kind of world the Christian is to go with "good news." What is this "good news" we are to embrace and to proclaim? What is it that should give us abiding joy and peace of heart?

We speak of the gospel as being the "good news." What is it that is good news? What is the gospel? Dr. John Marsh offers stimulating thoughts as we look at this gospel.

In the first place, the gospel can be seen as history. The account of the gospel is given to us in what we know as the four Gospels—Matthew, Mark, Luke, and John. It is the account of what took place when Jesus, the Christ, came to earth. It is God's action in history when, at a point of time, in a certain place, he, in the form of man, came to earth. The accounts of this event are given by these four writers.

In the second place, when we read in one of the Gospels what actually took place, something else is taking place. It is not just a story but what God is doing through events. The gospel is a story which points to an event but also points to the meaning behind the event. It tells us what people are saying about this event, that "God was in Christ reconciling the world to himself," and that through this act, he has given us a word of reconciliation, a means whereby we might be brought to God.

The Bible throughout is concerned with a society, a people, always life in the people, the people of God. The Word is not just in isolation, but in company. The New Testament speaks to a community. And when the evangelist tells the story about Jesus, it is what God has done for the people. It is something which has taken place; it is the news about what has taken place. God has now remade human life, wholly with the purpose of God.

The "good news" speaks to them about their own situation, about the life of the people. It speaks to us, as persons immersed in a society, about our own situation, and this is why every new generation must have a reinterpretation of the gospel for its age, a theology for the given situation. To be sure, the gospel does not change, but the age to which it speaks does, and this Word must be slanted to contemporary life in each generation.

Now in the third place, what does this good news

consist of? For one thing, it tells us that there is no possibility of man being able to establish this divine community on his own. This kingdom of God cannot be brought in by man himself. If there is to be a community of God and man, the dominant factor must be God—the creator and ruler of life. Man must come to him in total self-commitment.

A demonstration of this was given to us in the gospel story by our Lord coming and giving himself completely to God. The religious man saw in this act a threat. But God is telling us through the gospel story that this is the only way new life can begin— man giving himself completely to God. So when we read from the four Gospels, we do not just read a story, but also we see how God has established earth and men to have fellowship with him.

"We now see through a glass darkly," but there is hope. Here is something that happened to Jesus and that happens to man. Here is a story with a meaning beyond itself. It is in parable. The reign of God finally began in Christ, but this is a parable for everyone else. It is what is to take place over and over again.

This is the good news that makes some of us run away. We are afraid to trust him, to live as he wants us to live. So we separate ourselves from God. We wander in the far country, estranged from the Father. It is good news that is almost too good to be true, so we run away. But it also tells us that this *love* of God will in the end win the world. We cannot live without it. It is at the very heart of life.

Thus, this means that we take our stand upon history. It all happened. It is a fact. We can read the accounts in Scripture. It is anchored in time. We can look back to the event. Some who are so fortunate can go and see where it all happened.

But there is more here than just history. For this history has a meaning. The whole line of Christianity has a meaning. The events that occurred are not justified merely in facts but by what these facts mean. The Resurrection is not just resuscitation, not a life brought back as was Lazarus, but it is God acting in and beyond history. We are sinful men and need to be brought under judgment. This is the good news of what God has done for us in Jesus Christ. When this new life goes on beyond, it tells us that Jesus now lives and is at the right hand of God. He is now in the world with us and also in the life of the Christian church. He lives now in part through the life of people in the church. He is alive and at work in our midst.

It makes us know that we need not despair, that God is at work in our midst, and that we can trust him to be like the Jesus of Scripture, for in him God lived and moved. We are to try to be like him, the Christ, and to commit our lives into his care and keeping.

Thus, "God was in Christ reconciling the world to himself."

AIDS TO WORSHIP

Hymns: "The Church's One Foundation"
          "My Hope Is Built on Nothing Less"
Scripture: II Cor. 5

A PRAYER

Eternal God, before whose majesty and power we stand in awe and yet in whose presence we call thee Father, we raise to thee our grateful praise.

Through all the mystery of life help us to see behind it and in it a great God. In all the immensity of space and the unfathomable worlds about us, help us to affirm, like our fathers before us, "Before the mountains were brought forth, or ever thou hadst formed the earth and the world, from everlasting to everlasting thou art God."

Confront us, O God, with the truth that in all the mystery of life and the immensity of space, we have a special place in thy concern.

Give us contrite hearts for our sins and thankful hearts for thy forgiveness. Lure us toward the ideal of manhood thou hast set before us, but remind us that thou dost accept us as we are—imperfect children. In Christ's name we pray. Amen.

4

What Would We Do with Jesus?

Oftentimes men wonder what Jesus would do were he to return to the earth in the flesh. Would he feel at home here? Would our modern churches please him? Would he feel that we represent him well as believing Christians to an unbelieving world?

But a more searching question than "What would Jesus do?" is "What would we do with Jesus?"

In the first place, if Jesus were to return now, we would feel uncomfortable in his presence. We would feel uncomfortable because we would be made vividly aware of the gap between his manhood and ours— for here would be perfect man confronting sinful man. We would be awed by him.

When we turn back to the days when Jesus was on earth, Luke tells us that after Simon Peter had come to know Jesus, had had him in his own house, he "fell down at Jesus' knees, saying, 'Depart from me, for I am a sinful man, O Lord.'" This may seem at first to be a strange way to react to the beauty and strength of Jesus, but it is a natural response when one really sees him, sees him in all of his strength and greatness. It is to take him seriously. This happens to us whenever we are confronted with perfection as against our imperfection. We feel so small in the presence of greatness.

When we take the character and teachings of the Master seriously, which of us does not feel dwarfed? "Depart from me. They are beyond my grasp or reach," we cry. It is disturbing to be confronted with perfection. Jesus is the most disturbing personality a man ever faces. Instinctly, we do not run to him but try to escape him because we know that within our own feeble selves his ways are beyond our ways and his thoughts beyond our thoughts. But let us not stop here.

In the second place, if we look long enough and deep enough, we see beyond his manhood to God. If Jesus were to return, would we just feel unworthy and uncomfortable in his presence? Would the matter end there with despair? We find our answer in the New Testament, for these early disciples not only felt uncomfortable, crying out, "Depart from me," but they went beyond this and discovered that in Jesus there was more than perfect man. God was there, too. Here was the Eternal being expressed in time. Simon Peter saw this in Christ, and he saw hope. He saw that God through Christ could enter into his life, too. In later years Peter wrote in one of the epistles: "The God of all grace, who has called you to his eternal glory in Christ, will himself restore, establish, strengthen you." This is it!

When we keep our gaze upon Jesus and look long enough, we soon see more than perfect man—we see the eternal God, who came down to earth as the Savior of mankind. To the first Christians Jesus was the "word made flesh," and meant for them that God was very near, making himself known and making himself available. Here was their hope! From despair they found this hope in him. Peter started by saying, "Depart from me, for I am a sinful man," and ended by saying, "Thou art the Christ, the Son of the living God." This is what happens to us if we gaze long enough on him.

Thus, to be confronted by Jesus Christ is humbling and yet inspiring and uplifting. This happens to us when we truly worship him. It humbles us and then exalts us. It makes us aware of our own sins and yet places us in the presence of one who can free us from the burden of our sins. To gaze upon him not only reveals our shortcomings but also inspires us to be and to do better. We come away renewed and inspired.

Finally, if Jesus were to return, we would be made aware that here is the Savior offering to set us free, but more, here he is commissioning us to go out into all the world and serve him. If he were to return, our churches would have to measure their work by him— his teachings, his spirit, his mission.

The real measurement of a church is how it measures up to the mind and spirit of Christ. There was once a man who was trying to fit a painting of a great artist into his room. He complained that he didn't seem to get it to fit. Then, some discerning soul said, "Sir, you cannot get the picture to fit the room; you must make the room fit the picture."

So with the church. Jesus should not be made to fit our churches, but rather we should seek to make our churches fit him.

To fit his spirit the church must reach out beyond its own borders to men and women everywhere with a mission. As James D. Smart reminds us,

The early church was not an institution but rather a mission, a bold and seemingly fantastic mission as a little group of Jews set out to claim the whole world for their Lord, Jesus Christ. Whenever it ceased to be a mission and has become content to be merely a religious institution, it has withered and died. But again and again it has happened that out of the dry shell a new missionary impulse has broken forth with important consequences for the world.

AIDS TO WORSHIP

Hymns: "Lord, Speak to Me, That I May Speak"
"Take My Life and Let It Be"
Scripture: I Pet. 5:1-11

A PRAYER

Almighty God, who hast caused the light of life to come forth out of darkness, with songs of joy and hearts filled with gratitude we pause in thy presence this day.

We thank thee for thy love which gave us Jesus Christ, our Lord. We thank thee for his earthly life, for the temptations he faced, for his perfect manhood. We

31

thank thee for his victory over death and for his sacrifices that we might know thy love and the saving power of his resurrection.

We thank thee that nothing can separate us from the love of Christ—tribulation, distress, persecution, famine, nakedness, peril, or sword. We are grateful to believe that thy love for us cannot be destroyed whatever we do. Help us, we pray, to accept ourselves and thy acceptance of us.

Meet us this day in the secret places of our souls. Walk through the hidden rooms of our hearts. Open the closets we have kept closed because of shame. Take from us all that is low and selfish, evil and of mean report, and lift up all that is beautiful and good, unselfish and of good report, through Jesus Christ, our Lord. Amen.

5
Teach Us to Pray

Long ago Augustine wrote, "Thou hast made us for thyself, and our hearts are restless until they rest in thee." This is another way of saying that we are homesick for God, from whom we come, and for whom we have been made. On every hand today we see this homesickness of the soul for God. It is given expression in the mad rush men make for happiness and pleasure, many times in a round of meaningless activity. The outward actions of people indicate that there is great need for an inward adventure which would add meaning and purpose to life.

If it is true that we are homesick for God, then our answer depends on communication with him. As friendships depend on frequent communications, so it is with God.

We are often the careless passersby in the use of prayer. We talk about it, think about it, and perhaps even admit that it sounds reasonable and say that we believe in it, but too often we do nothing about it.

We know that the disciples, recognizing this power in Jesus' life, made this one request that he teach them to pray. Certainly they must have observed how, time and time again when Jesus would be exhausted from the day's work, he would go apart to pray; every time he returned from such an hour, he would come with renewed strength and power to face the problems before him. They knew that the secret of his life—his power, his perserverance, his love, his manhood—all centered on his prayer life.

The Gospels do not speak too much about Jesus' praying, yet we know that he must have prayed constantly. The carpenter of Nazareth exhausted himself under the weight of human suffering and sorrow and then renewed his strength by periods of silence in the hills above his home or beside the lake. We are told that a great while before day he would go apart to meditate and commune with God, and all night long in times of crisis he would stay alone under the stars with the Eternal. Surely the vast reservoirs of power stored up in these early vigils and midnight watches carried him through Gethsemane and Calvary.

Thus, these disciples could feel their weaknesses and failures as compared to the strength of this man. They knew that without this power in their own lives, they could not follow his way. The fulfillment of his commands was dependent upon power beyond themselves. And Jesus' answer to their request has come down to us through the centuries and stands as the central prayer of our faith.

In answering their request, "Lord, teach us to pray," he suggested that they pray "after this man-

ner," or in this way. Why did he give them words
with which to pray? Perhaps it was because they were
likely to forget the things about which they should
pray; too, it may have been that he knew that they
would often be wearied of life and would need words
to repeat which might serve as a sort of trellis for
their own prayers upon which their spirits could
climb toward God.

He did not intend to give them a mere formula
which was to be repeated over and over, but rather
he was stating the principles which underlie the true
relationship between God and man which prayer
expresses. He gave them an idea of what prayer really
is and what people should pray for rather than a
prayer to be repeated in public and private devotions.
It was to be used as a means of communion with
God rather than a bit of verse to be repeated over
and over again.

In the Lord's Prayer Jesus describes the spirit
in which we are to pray. In it we find him telling us that we must pray with a sense of cooperation
with God. Prayer for us is not the bending of God's
will to ours, not asking favors as if he were a child's
Santa Claus, but the opening of our spirits to God,
so that we may understand his purposes. It is not
asking God to change his world to suit our own
selfish desires, nor giving God his orders for the day.
It is not a lifeboat to be launched only in an
emergency, not magic to get what we want.

Prayer is essentially relating and adjusting ourselves to God and his purposes. "Prayer," as Tennyson put it, "is like opening a sluice gate between the great ocean and our little channels, when the sea gathers itself together and flows in at full tide." In its highest expression it is communion and fellowship with God; herein lies its chief value—the relationship itself. The very heart of Jesus' prayer is summed up in these words: "Our Father, thy kingdom come, thy will be done." The answer he gave his disciples shows that Jesus did not desire "much speaking" but a right attitude to God and man.

Since Jesus' day the testimony as to the power of prayer has been given by many people. Henry M. Stanley, who faced the jungles of Africa in search of Livingstone, says,

On all my expeditions prayer made me stronger than my non-praying companions. It did not blind my eyes or dull my mind or close my ears, but on the contrary it gave me confidence; it did more; it gave me joy and pride in my work and lifted me beautifully over the 1500 miles of forest tracks, eager to face the days of peril and fatigue.

AIDS TO WORSHIP

Hymns: "Savior, Like a Shepherd Lead Us"
       "Lord, for Tomorrow and Its Needs"
Scripture: Luke 11:1-13

A Prayer

O Lord God, whose strength is sufficient for all who lay hold on it, and in whose power it is to give life and to recall life, we are grateful for this moment to praise and to worship thee. We thank thee that the slender threads of our beings are now uncut, and still we can serve thee according to thy holy ways. Give us thankful hearts for life itself and help us know that thou art the strength of our days as well as the source of our being.

Forgive us, O Lord, for our forgetfulness and negligence. We have too often forgotten thee in the mad rush to get ahead. We have sinned in thy sight, intent upon our own selfish ways. We have stayed too long in the marketplace and neglected the quiet place. We have paid homage to a world of things and ignored the spiritual world. We have lived too long in the glare of the streets, and need to pull apart that we might rightly see. Take us this day and make us aware of the spiritual world, through Jesus Christ, our Lord. Amen.

6
To Pray Courageously

We find Jesus telling us to pray courageously. This implies a willingness to be spent, which means that we are not seeking primarily for special virtues just for the sake of possessing them, but rather we are interested in the task that needs to be done regardless of our own welfare.

Prayer is demanding. We must be willing to follow through with the light we receive. Jesus said, "What I tell you in the dark, utter in the light."

Fulton Oursler tells of his experience when he was a small boy, dressed in his Sunday best and warned by his mother not to leave the front steps.

"We'll be walking over to see your aunt," she promised.

He waited obediently until the baker's son came by and called him a sissy. Then little Fulton sprang from the steps and hit the baker's son on the ear. The baker's son pushed him into a mud puddle, splotching the white blouse with mud and leaving his stockings with a bloody hole in the knee.

Hopelessly he began to cry. When the ice cream man came by, forgetting his disobedience young

Fulton rushed into the house and asked his mother for a penny to buy ice cream. He said that he never forgot his mother's answer.

"Look at yourself! You're in no condition to ask for anything."

Oursler said that many a year passed after that incident before it dawned on him "that often when we ask help from God, we need to look at ourselves; we may be in no condition to ask him for anything."

He is saying in effect that many times God cannot answer our prayers because we are not ready for his answer or that we are in no condition to be used by God in his answer. This means that prayer requires cooperation on our part, that it is not just some easy, meaningless petition; rather that it is costly.

It is well for us to remind ourselves what Oursler's mother said to him, "Look at yourself! You're in no condition to ask for anything." Maybe we don't really want our prayer answered. Perhaps at times we are like Augustine, who once prayed, "O God, make me pure, but not just now."

When we pray, "Thy kingdom come," we must live like citizens of his kingdom and then give ourselves to making it real. Many times our prayers are answered by God in and through us. We become the agents of his will, the channels of his love. This makes prayer costly business.

Jesus also teaches us to pray believingly. He began his prayer with assurance and ended with reassurance, "Our Father. . . . For thine is the kingdom, and the power and the glory, forever." He tells us that God hears and answers every prayer that is offered to him, but God, like an earthly father, must often say "No" as well as "Yes." When we consider the partialness of our knowledge, "No" can sometimes be a kinder answer than "Yes."

As earthly parents dealing with little children, we give them not the things they ask for but what in our best judgment is best for them. So, Harry Emerson Fosdick reminds us that when we consider the partialness of our knowledge, the narrowness of our outlook, our little skill in tracing far-off consequences of our desires, we see how often God must speak to us as did Jesus to the ambitious woman, "You do not know what you are asking."

Often God answers our prayers in a way we do not expect and perhaps do not like. Henry Ward Beecher spoke of this when he said, "A woman prays for patience and God sends her a green cook." We seek a thing and God gives us a chance.

The mother of Augustine, Monica, prayed all night in a seaside chapel on the northern coast of Africa that God would not let her son sail for Italy. She wanted him to become a Christian. But he did sail and came under the influence of the preaching of Bishop Ambrose in Milan and was converted. God denied the form of her prayer but granted its substance.

Thus, when we pray we open our minds and hearts to God, and look at our lives and the world from a new viewpoint, and find new power and strength to face life again. When Jesus "rose and went out to a lonely place" and prayed, it is here that we find the secret of his power and the renewal of that power. Behind his whole public ministry, when great crowds were gathered around him, when matchless words came forth from his lips, when men and women were given new hope in life—behind it all was this private solitude.

For Jesus it was not a time out for prayer. It was rather a time for the renewal of life, for fresh adjustment to the will of God. It was a time for replenishment of the power of God. Here new energies flowed into his life. Here the weariness which had overtaken him gave way to renewed strength. Indeed, rather than being a time out for prayer, it was the most important time which he spent.

So, for Jesus going out to a lonely place and praying was not a passive act but the highest activity of mind and spirit. Sometime ago I passed a young forest of trees which had been planted years ago. It was a lovely scene. The pines were tall and straight and underneath was a soft bed of needles. Along the highway was this sign: "Quiet, Trees at Work." Nothing seemed to be happening, but these trees were busy at work, quietly, silently opening themselves to the unseen forces of their environment.

And this can be for us the secret of life and of power—opening our souls to the unseen force of our environment, God.

AIDS TO WORSHIP

Hymns: "Dear Lord and Father of Mankind"
"Savior, Like a Shepherd Lead Us"
Scripture: Luke 20:20-28

A Prayer

O God, thou hast given us another day to worship thee. Make this, we pray, a hallowed hour. We know thou art incomprehensible in thy mysterious greatness, and yet dost reveal thyself to us in so many ways. We would be still now and listen to thy voice as thou dost speak to us. We come assured that thou art ready to meet us at our point of deepest need.

There are decisions to be made, which affect not only our lives but the lives of others. There are commitments that have to be made, to make more of life than now we are doing. There are chains of sins which need to be broken by the power of thy love. We need to start afresh and leave behind old ways of living.

Help us this day to be dissatisfied with ourselves, with the thoughts we are thinking, with the deeds we are doing, with the life we are living. Help us to know that we can be bigger and better than we are. Help us to be pleasant with those around us, to be willing to take our share of the load, to bear with fortitude the trials that come our way. Help us to lose ourselves in the work thou hast given us to do.

Give us the desire to be about "the Father's business," and the strength and will to do it. Amen.

7
When a Man Comes to Himself

Man's chief job in life is to be himself—that is, what God intended him to be. The great struggle in life is trying to be the type persons we were intended to be. Surely within the heart of every man is the desire to make good, to be a success as a human being. But the tragedy is that so many of us miss the bus, take the wrong road, and too late discover our misdirection. The question we may well ask ourselves is, "When does a man come to himself?"

Jesus was talking about men finding themselves when he told the story of the prodigal son. You recall how the young man took his share of the father's fortune and left for the far country, soon to discover that his selected road led to emptiness. He went from bad to worse, living like swine, following what he thought would bring satisfaction. Jesus spoke of him thusly, "But when he came to himself," or as Moffatt translates it, "But when he came to his senses."

In the first place, we find the prodigal son came to his senses when he discovered his own inadequacy. He felt sufficient and wandered into a far country leaving his father behind. Like so many people today, he felt no need for help other than his own. Of course he would take his share of the fortune, which he considered as being his just due, but after that he would be on his own. By and by, you remember, he forgot his father's teachings and lost all that he had. Life began to close in around him. Futilely he reached out for help from his friends, who long since had deserted him because he had spent all and had nothing to offer them.

Suddenly, in a moment of despair, he saw himself for the first time as a broken man needing strength that only his father could give. Jesus said it was then that he came to himself. "I will arise and go to my father."

So it is in the life of each one of us. We come to ourselves when we discover that we need God to sustain us, to uphold us in all our undertakings.

In the second place, each man comes to himself, as the prodigal son came, when he finds himself in God's world, when he discovers his place in the scheme of things—what God intended for his life.

Woodrow Wilson once wisely said, "A man comes to himself after experiences of which he alone may be aware; when he has left off being wholly preoccupied with his own powers and interests and with every petty plan that centers in himself; when he has cleared his eyes to see the world as it is, and his own true place and function in it."

He then discovers that he lives in a world in which

he did not make the rules. A man comes to himself when he discovers that he does not make the laws of life—they are made for him, and his happiness and destiny will depend upon his ability to live inside the law.

In Harold B. Walker's book *Power to Manage Yourself*, there is the story of a hillbilly who made a great reputation as a marksman. Other woodsmen who followed him found rings marked with chalk on trees and posts. In the center of each ring was a bullet hole. One day a man asked him the secret of his skill. "That's easy," he said, "I just shoot the hole and then go draw the ring around it."

Many there are who, like the hillbilly, undertake to make the rules of life to suit themselves. This was the trouble with the prodigal. He thought he could make his own rules in the far country, away from the father's house, and what he had learned to be true about life would not catch up with him. Many today when they have sinned do not repent, but invent a code of conduct that justifies their sinning. Then they live as if their rule were the divine law of life.

It is a sign of growth when a man learns that he does not make the laws of life, that they are made for him, and that if life is to be full and good he must adjust to those laws.

In the third place, a man comes to himself when he discovers that life is "to give and not to take." Some see life as what they can get from it; others, what they can give to it. Woodrow Wilson said a "man who lives only for himself has not begun to live—has yet to learn his use, and his pleasure, too, in the world." It is in service to others, forgetting self, wherein a man discovers his true nature. Love is the dominant note. Self-satisfaction in life does not come with self as the object, but rather through service to others.

A man comes to himself when he ceases to think only about himself and is concerned with others. It is when he loses himself in something greater than himself that he comes of age; it is when life ceases to be something to get and becomes something to give; it is when the drive in his life is more than just getting ahead; it is when he has some fine reason for living; it is when he is committed to some cause outside himself to which he gives himself and in which he loses himself, that he really finds himself. It is when personal gain gives way to right; it is when personal interest gives way to public welfare; it is when a man does not ask a privilege for himself which he is not willing to give another; it is when a man wants freedom not only for himself but for all men, that he comes to himself.

It is when a man discovers himself to be part of the family of God that he wants to dwell in the Father's house and in the Father's world; it is when he says, "I will arise and go to my father"; it is when he sees all men as members of the household of God; it is when he feels kinship to the Father's children;

it is when he identifies himself as belonging to the family of God, that he comes to himself.

What happens, then, when a man comes to himself? He begins to live. Life becomes an adventure for God. "This my son was dead and is alive again." He finds the purpose for which he is made—finding and doing the will of God.

This is all another way of saying that conversion to the Christian faith brings man to himself. It brings the soul to itself as well as to God. This is God's world and we are his creatures, and when we discover this and find ourselves within his world, then we come to ourselves.

AIDS TO WORSHIP

Hymns: "A Charge to Keep I Have"
        "Lord, Speak to Me"
Scripture: Luke 15:11-32

A PRAYER

O God, in whose presence we come and by whose power we live, we bow before thee, the creator and sustainer of life.

From the rush and hurry of the world we come; from the noise of the marketplace we would pause and be still and know that thou art God. In our search for happiness and satisfaction in life we seek thy way and thy truth. Give to us a sure word, a comforting thought, a challenging faith. Help us to find an answer to our quest for meaning in life. Push back the curtain of time that we might get a glimpse of eternity.

Anchor us in thy truth;
uphold us by thy might;
strengthen us in our faith;
secure us in our future.

Not only for ourselves would we pray, but for people everywhere—the lonely, the suffering, the abused, the imprisoned. Be with all who are living in the shadows of darkness and ignorance, all who are enslaved to evil habit, all who are victims of persecution and violence, all whose hearts have been saddened by death.

Give to us victory in our faith and gladness of heart because we are thy children. Help us to rejoice in thy love and mercy made known in Christ, and in his name we pray. Amen.

8
Accept Yourself—God Does

The last verse of the fifth chapter of Matthew challenges us with these words: "You, therefore, must be perfect, as your heavenly Father is perfect." Now these words seem to command us to be like God in perfection, and yet we know that we are made of clay, finite in all areas of life. How then can we be perfect as our Father in heaven is perfect?

This is a question that continually haunts us, especially those of sensitive frames. On the one hand we may demand for ourselves a perfection which on the other we know is impossible. Can we, frail dust, be perfect? Are we not tormented by our perversity? We burn our fingers a hundred times on the same fire and wrestle with a guilty past. Perfection—far from it!

J. B. Phillips points up the problem by saying,

Of all the false gods there is probably no greater nuisance in the spiritual world than the "god of one hundred percent." . . . It can be so easily argued that since God is Perfection, and since He asks the complete loyalty of His creatures, then the best way of serving, pleasing, and worshipping Him is to set up absolute one-hundred-percent standards and see to it that we obey them. After all, did not Christ say, "Be ye perfect"?

But he also points out for us that this menace to Christians in all schools of thought has led quite a number of sensitive, conscientious people to what is called a "nervous breakdown." And, too, it has taken spontaneity out of the Christian life for many. To be sure, there are those extroverts who talk glibly of the absolutes, the "one-hundred-percent pure, honest, loving, and unselfish." Yet they haven't the slightest idea of what real perfection means. What they really mean by one-hundred-percent perfection is that they will do the best they know how, which of course is far from perfection.

Certainly the church is far from perfect; Jesus recognized this when he selected his twelve—men of human frame, frail as dust, imperfect, yet striving for the ideal. Look at them: James and John and Matthew and Philip and Thomas and all the others, and then Peter who denied him, and Judas who betrayed him. He knew how imperfect they all were, and he would have never founded his church had he waited for the perfect set of people to start it.

But all this is not to say that we shouldn't strive for the highest and attempt to reach our high goals. It is to say that we can never reach perfection, that the Christian ethic is always beyond our reach, and the nearer we approach it, the farther away it seems to us.

What then are we to do? How are we to interpret this text: "You, therefore, must be perfect, as your heavenly Father is perfect"?

In the first place, the perfection toward which Jesus is urging us on is one of growth toward the ideal. It is the steady, upward progress toward the ideal, and that ideal is found in Christ. When Christ said, "Learn of me," he implied that we should grow like him. We should press toward the mark.

But how do we resolve this apparent contradiction of trying to be perfect when we are imperfect, of trying to mount up with wings, and are still caught fast in ignorant clay?

"You . . . must be perfect" implies that we were never intended to climb the mountain in our own strength. George Buttrick tells us that

failure comes to teach us that life is an affair, not of man alone or of man with man, but of man with God and God with man. The word Father is the key to the Sermon on the Mount. There the ethic breaks into faith and comradeship. There we find forgiveness and new power—and life's secret meaning. Thus "as your Father which is in heaven is perfect" sums up the new law and the new life.

In the second place, it tells us too that though God is perfection, he is no perfectionist. He is interested in all of us who cannot be anything else but imperfection. If he were not interested in anything but perfection, indeed the whole human race would be in a sorry plight. To be sure, he desires that all his children give him our devotion and loyalty, but he is interested in us whether we give him this devotion or not.

Don't you see what this means? God cares about the likes of you and me. We can never wander beyond his loving care nor out of reach of his brooding compassion for us. We are welcome in his church whether we commit one kind of sin or another. Our spiritual condition does not determine his love for us. His love is not determined by the pigment of our skin, the status of our social standing, or the balance of our bank accounts. His love is all-embracing and unchanging. It does not alter with life's changing moods nor fluctuate with the accident of our birth.

Don't you see what this means? It all means that if God accepts us as human beings and as children of his, who are we not to accept ourselves? God accepts us just as we are, with no changes, no improvements, no alterations. We are his and he is ours.

To be sure, he would have us strive toward the goals he holds out before us. He would tempt us to be better than we are, but he knows that we can never be the way he wants us to be unless we rely on his power and his grace to see us through. God is forever pulling us toward his ideal, toward his perfection. He is not asking us to reach it, for this we cannot do, but he is asking us to be growing toward it, to be reaching upward.

"You, therefore, must be perfect, as your heavenly Father is perfect."

AIDS TO WORSHIP

Hymns: "Holy Spirit, Faithful Guide"
　　　　"There's a Wideness in God's Mercy"
Scripture: Matt. 5:38-48

A Prayer

Eternal God, in whose presence we come, and by whose power and grace we live, this is the day that thou hast made; help us to be joyous in it.

We confess our lack of faith and trust:

　　our cowardice in the face of danger;
　　our weakness in confronting temptation;
　　our timidity in the presence of evil; and
　　our indifference before thy claims upon us.

Lift us, we pray:

　　to higher levels of thinking and living;
　　to new insights of truth and goodness;
　　to new hopes and dreams of a better life;
　　to new strength in facing the demands of living.

Save us from weak resignation to the evils we deplore, and set our feet upon foundations whose builder and maker is God. We wait before thee, assured that thou knowest best what is good for us to do and to dare. Make known thy way and give us the will and grace to walk therein. Amen.

9
To Live Is to Suffer

In finding the real meaning of life one discovers that suffering is a part of our lot. This we cannot escape. To live is to suffer. Therefore, if life is to be meaningful, we need desperately to find a place for suffering in it and to try to discover how to cope with it.

Viktor Frankl in his book *Man's Search for Meaning* tells us that "to live is to suffer and to survive is to find meaning in suffering." He says that of great significance is the attitude we take toward suffering, "the attitude in which we take our suffering upon ourselves."

He speaks out of trying experiences of years spent as a Nazi prisoner in a concentration camp—Auschwitz. He, a noted doctor of medicine and a psychiatrist, was arrested and stripped of all identity as an Austrian Jew. He became No. 119,104. "As a longtime prisoner in bestial concentration camps," Dr. Gordon Allport of Harvard says, "he found himself stripped to naked existence. His father, mother, brother, and his wife died in camps or were sent to the gas ovens, so that, excepting for his sister, his entire family perished in these camps." His chance of survival was one in twenty. So out of these experiences, too deep for deception, he learned a lot about life and suffering.

He discovered that "suffering ceases to be suffering in some way at the moment it finds meaning, such as the meaning of a sacrifice." He feels that man's "main concern is not to gain pleasure or to avoid pain, but rather to see a meaning in his life. That is why man is even ready to suffer, on the condition, to be sure, that his suffering has a meaning."

He cites the case of a doctor, a general practitioner, who came to him for help. This doctor was in great despair over the loss of his wife. His grief was almost more than he could bear.

Dr. Frankl then asked him this question, "What would have happened, Doctor, if you had died first, and your wife would have had to survive you?" "Oh," he said, "for her this would have been terrible; how she would have suffered!"

Then Dr. Frankl replied, "You see, Doctor, such a suffering has been spared her, and it was you who have spared her this suffering; but now, you have to pay for it by surviving and mourning her." This seemed to help, as the doctor without a word shook his hand and quietly left his office.

Suffering in a sense ceases to be unbearable suffering when it finds a meaning, such as a sacrifice. A mother will go through untold hardship for the sake of her child. A father will do without so that his family may have the necessities of life. An unhappy workman will continue on his unimaginative job so that his son might get an education. Men and women will leave home and much of what they hold dear to go on perilous journeys to far-off lands as missionaries, if they see some meaning in life and some purpose in what they are doing.

Deprivation and suffering lose some of their sting if there is some reason for them, if some meaning can be seen. In our Bible we read, "Pagans waste their pain." Could this not mean, among other things, that they see no meaning or sacrifice in it? I wonder if the agony of the cross was withstood by Jesus partially because he saw some meaning in it. He said, "And I, when I am lifted up . . . will draw all men to myself." His suffering was not wasted. God used it even for his purpose.

Perhaps, in our suffering, even when we can see no good in it and it is void of apparent meaning, the cross of Christ and all the suffering it represents can help us bear our own. Jesus prayed in the garden, "Father, all things are possible to thee; remove this cup from me; yet not what I will, but what thou wilt." But there seemed to be no other way but suffering for him, and then with confidence he prayed on the cross, "Father, into thy hands I commend my spirit." In our suffering Christ is very near to us, in compassion and in understanding. He can help us bear our own.

Roy A. Burkhart, with rare insight, says in his book *The Person You Can Be* that "every problem is either solvable or transcendable." He calls our attention to the life of Helen Keller, who became blind and deaf at nineteen months of age. Her problem was not solvable but she was able to transcend it. Jesus prayed to escape his cup, but it did not pass; he transcended it, turning defeat into victory. "He did not escape his cross, but he had the power and strength to make it the world's greatest throne."

Viktor Frankl tells us that "man is not fully conditioned and determined but rather determines himself whether he gives in to conditions or stands up to them. . . . One of the main features of human existence is the capacity to rise above such conditions and transcend them." It is God who gives us this power to overcome. Remember this in your suffering!

Let us remember Jesus' words, "My grace is sufficient for you." Such strength and help from God, the Father, through Christ can help us transcend our suffering and live nobly in spite of it.

AIDS TO WORSHIP

Hymns: "O God, Our Help in Ages Past"
       "The Lord Is My Shepherd"
Scripture: John 12:23-36

A Prayer

O God, our Father, whose love has never let us go and beyond whose brooding care we cannot drift, we would quiet our souls in thy presence and rest ourselves in the confidence of thy sustaining strength, that the peace of God which passeth all understanding may guard our hearts and thoughts.

Through countless channels thou dost seek our lives, at many a door thou dost stand and knock. We wait now for thy still small voice which can change our fear to faith and our cowardice to courage.

Grant to us faith in thee, that in the face of life's illness and trials we may share Jesus' trustful, confident mind, and be freed from the cares which destroy us. Grant us his unfaltering belief in thy goodness, that whether pain or joy be our lot, we may still know ourselves to be upheld by thy strength. In his name we pray. Amen.

10
Compassion and Humility

Art Linkletter had as a guest on one of his television programs Bishop Herbert Welch, retired Methodist bishop who had just reached one hundred years of age. He is a most remarkable man and has published his autobiography on observations during his first hundred years.

Art Linkletter asked him on this program what he considered the greatest needs of our time. It is interesting to note that he listed two. First, the bishop said that the world needed *compassion*, and second, *humility*. He said that by compassion he did not mean pity, but deep concern and understanding.

I guess there is no greater need in human relations today than compassion. There is so much in life that hurts and bruises men; there is so much sorrow and suffering; there is so much evil that crushes men. To have compassion is to look with concern and deep feeling upon the wounds of men. It is to know that but for the grace of God many of us would be where others are—in unwanted circumstances.

We all know what it means to have someone by

our side to say "I understand!" To understand is to have compassion. It is not to condemn, but to reach out in concern and love. Oftentimes I think of the wise words of Ian Maclaren, who once said, "Let us be kind to one another for most of us are fighting a hard battle."

To have compassion is not only to reach out in understanding and concern, but it is also to reach out offering help. Love always goes beyond feeling to action. To be sure, the priest and Levite felt sorry for the wounded wayfarer, but it was the good Samaritan who not only felt sorry but who reached out in compassionate action, who did something about the wounded man. Here was action. Genuine compassion never passes by in unconcern.

Again, Bishop Welch lifts up the great need for humility in our world today. This is to acknowledge that God is the creator and ruler of life, and that all that we have and are we owe to him. It is to recognize that we are utterly dependent upon him not only for the chance to live but for life here and now. It is to be grateful to God for this life which has been lent us. It is to so live as to do honor to him who gave us life. It is to be grateful for all that comes to us from his great mercy and love.

The opposite of humility is pride, and C. S. Lewis writes that "pride leads to every other vice; it is the complete anti-God state of mind. . . . Pride is spiritual cancer; it eats up the very possibility of love, or contentment, or even common sense." The writer of

Proverbs puts it like this: "Pride goes before destruction, and a haughty spirit before a fall."

When a person becomes intoxicated with his own achievements and closes his mind to new truth, then he is headed for a fall. The proud man closes his mind and resists God because he is too proud to receive new truth.

To the humble God gives grace and truth. This is what Thomas Huxley had in mind when he wrote Charles Kingsley: "Sit down before the facts as a little child, and be prepared to give up every preconceived notion; follow humbly wherever Nature leads, or you shall learn nothing. I have only begun to learn content and peace of mind since I resolved at all risks to do this."

The humble person is the grateful person. The proud always take life for granted, always expecting more to come their way. But the humble, feeling they do not deserve much from God, see his goodness in the smallest blessing. The humble person is the thankful person, and the thankful person is the happy person.

Pride breeds a sense of self-sufficiency. The world is my oyster. I owe no man anything. I do not need God's help. I can run my own show. I feel no need of religion. But self-sufficiency is the shoal on which many a promising life has been wrecked.

The humble recognize their dependence upon others for success and especially upon God.

AIDS TO WORSHIP

Hymns: "Breathe on Me, Breath of God"
   "I Would Be True"
Scripture: Luke 10:25-37

A Prayer

Eternal God, in whose presence we come this day, and by whose power and grace we live, we thank thee for these moments of quietness wherein we may be still and know that thou art God.

From the rush and hurry of daily life we pause to acknowledge thee as the Lord of life, and to seek from thee help for the days ahead. We need thee, O God, to help us where we live and to strengthen us in doing thy will in the world.

Help us to be kind with those we meet, to recognize all men as children of thine. Keep us pure when we are tempted to do evil. Give us courage when we are tempted to be cowardly. Hold our tongues when we would speak ill of anyone. Give us faith and trust and love that would drive out fear and anxiety. Hold us in thy hand and help us know that in thee is our assurance. In Christ's name we pray. Amen.

11
Candles to Be Lighted

Now and then someone tells me that they want a job in the church—that they want to become active. Of course, the church does need leaders—teachers, stewards, singers, class officers, greeters, scout leaders, youth workers, visitors, committee chairmen, committee members, ushers, collectors, typists, and many others to fill places that have to be manned. Indeed, the church could not run without a host of faithful workers.

But in a real sense every member has a job as a follower of Christ, and that job is defined in the sixteenth verse of the fifth chapter of Matthew: "Let your light so shine before men, that they may see your good works and give glory to your Father who is in heaven."

This is our commission—to be a light that shines, a candle that burns, a life which adds glory to God's name. The fact is there are not enough titled jobs to go around in the organization of the church, and just to create jobs and to formulate titles can be a hollow sort of thing. But there is something for everyone to do—to be a light that shines, a witness for God. Everyone can be active—an active disciple of

Christ in seeking to spread his good news to men everywhere. We come to church and Sunday school to learn of God as we know him in Christ and to be inspired to love and serve him.

In the first place, this verse from Matthew suggests that each one of us is a candle to be lighted. "Let your light so shine before men." These lives of ours remain dark in outlook and in purpose until God is let in and lights them. We are indeed unlighted candles, people with unimaginable possibilities, that God is waiting to light.

In the first chapter of the Fourth Gospel we find Jesus facing a man not unlike many of us. Here we see him looking into the face of Simon and discovering an unlighted candle. He looks beneath the surface and says, "You are Simon," an unlettered fisherman. You are impulsive, and an untrue friend. Your life means little now. But he doesn't stop here but says to this man, "You are Peter, and on this rock I will build my church." You shall be a lighted candle whose rays shall heal those upon whom they fall. You shall be a tower of strength upon whom men shall lean.

Here we see Jesus looking beyond the mere exterior of Simon and seeing beneath his crudeness vast undeveloped possibilities. He sees a light which is dark but which can be made to shine. This is what he sees in each of us—a candle which can give light. We find him spending the greater part of his ministry lighting candles, calling out of men their best, recognizing their faults and failures, but challenging them to something better.

History is replete with men whose lives have turned from darkness to light, whose latent possibilities have been released.

In the second place, Jesus is here telling us that God judges our little candles not only by the light they are now giving but by what they can give. "Let your light so shine before men, that they may see your good works and give glory to your Father who is in heaven." Of course, Jesus looks at these lives of ours and recognizes their limits, their present condition, knowing that tomorrow is determined by today. But he goes beyond to what we may become. "You are Simon," he says, "but you can become Peter."

Each of us is made up of two parts—what we are and what we may become. Regardless of our age and station in life, these divisions remain with us. Our concern should be not so much with what we now are, but what under God we may become. It is not so much the actuality today but the potentiality of tomorrow with which we are concerned. It is tragic to see so many lives today which are dark, which are not fulfilling the purposes for which they were made. But God can take a life and transform it.

Here is the life of Wilfred Grenfell, whose brilliance in the medical world had already gained recognition. To be sure, he was doing useful tasks, but there were vast undeveloped potentialities in his life.

One night in London God spoke to Grenfell through the voice of Dwight L. Moody and said, "Wilfred, I want you to be a lighted candle for me in a far-off land which is cold and very dark." And God made his life immortal in Labrador.

Finally, to "let your light so shine, that men may see your good works," not only helps you to find life's purpose, but also "gives glory to your Father who is in heaven." To shine as a ray of light in a darkened world glorifies God because the purpose for which we were made is being fulfilled.

It is reasonable to believe that he who made us wants to possess us, wants us to be that for which we were intended. What is God's will for my life? That is the question and the most important one in life. The discovery of it is the beginning of all wisdom. Unless we let God take hold of our lives and become their master, we are lost. God has a place for these lives of ours, and unless we give him full sway the purpose for their existence does not become realized.

Roy Pearson in the foreword of his book *The Ministry of Preaching* puts it like this: "The author adds his little candle to the lights burning around him, and he hopes he has not increased the shadows on the wall." So may it be with us!

AIDS TO WORSHIP

Hymns: "O Jesus, I Have Promised"
       "Walk in the Light"
Scripture: Matt. 5:1-16

A Prayer

O God, who bestowest thy mercy at all times on them that love thee, and in no place art distant from those that serve thee, quicken within us a sense of thy holy presence.

We come this day confessing that we have not loved thee as we ought to have loved thee; we have done those things which we ought not to have done and we have left undone those things which should have been done. From our lips unkind words have been hastily spoken; in our minds unhealthy thoughts have been entertained; with our feet we have often followed paths of unrighteous living; with our hands we have given ourselves to unworthy tasks.

Call us back, we pray, to righteous living and to a closer walk with thee. Send us out as worthy witnesses for thee and as ambassadors of Christ, our king. Amen.

12

In the Light of God's Love

God knew that love is a language that everyone understands, so he sent Jesus into the world. In Jesus Christ we see the incarnation of love. He appeals to men of all ages, of all races, of all clans, because they see in him *love*.

There is no word in any tongue today that deserves more attention than this little word—*love*. The extent of its application in today's world determines the future of mankind. Basic in every marriage bond, essential in all lasting friendships, necessary in all relationships, this word holds the key to that brave new world of which we dream and toward which we strive.

It was because of this that Paul said, "so faith, hope, love abide, these three; but the greatest of these is love." Therefore, "Make love your aim." This is the supreme virtue.

Paul was right. Life's greatest virtue is love. And Jesus Christ is the incarnation of love, the highest expression of it we know, and he commanded his disciples that they should love one another. He insisted that his followers be known by their love for him and for one another. Jesus came not to lay down a set of rules for human behavior but to manifest a spirit, a new way of life. Without this spirit of love, life is incomplete, imperfect and defective.

Let us look at this love which completes life and crowns it.

In the first place, knowledge without love leads to evil ends and even destruction. Paul says, "If I have prophetic powers, and understand all mysteries and all knowledge . . . but have not love, I am nothing." He is telling us that knowledge, learning, and scientific progress avail for nothing unless at the heart there is good will toward all men. All knowledge and achievement count for nothing unless they are motivated by love.

How true his words are today! We have explored the mysteries of life. We have fashioned in laboratories that which can lengthen life. We have conquered the air with planes and the sea with ships and submarines. We have shortened space and to some degree lengthened time with our laborsaving devices. Our world has been squeezed into a neighborhood through the machine. A boy in the Air Force writing his mother said, "Up there the world looks so small and so much one."

Yet, what has happened? In our laboratories where vaccines have been produced to lengthen men's lives, we have produced gases which would shorten lives. Our planes which have conquered the air and have borne medicine and food for people in need now threaten the existence of millions. Where once they carried life, they now carry the possibility of death. Ships which connected continents and brought them closer together now have been used in our time to push them farther apart. Engineers who fashioned luxurious cars turned their skills to produce tanks of death.

Paul says that men may prophesy, understand all mysteries and knowledge, but unless there is love in the heart, that which they have made counts for nothing except destruction. It is not enough to gain wisdom, but that wisdom must be directed by a loving will.

In the second place, love completes and crowns every human relationship. There can be no neighborliness without love. The nations of the world will remain suspicious of one another until love brings them together.

Married life soon shipwrecks if it is not crowned with a steadier flame than romantic passions which bring people together. That steady flame is love which endures the hardships of life. Parenthood is a tender and precious relationship in life, but there will be continual misunderstandings between the generations until the gulf is bridged by love. Indeed, love crowns every human relationship and is a vital and urgent necessity for the world in which we live.

And finally, the future belongs to love. It belongs to love because love is a language everyone can understand and that everyone can speak if he will. This is why Henry Drummond wrote a little book about love and called it *The Greatest Thing in the World.*

Real love has a magic power. You can feel its healing influence; it has a presence all its own. You can tell when a person loves you and feels kindly toward you. It conveys a message even without words. It assumes an attitude. It radiates a warmth.

To love one has to first be loved. An old English priest used to pray "O God, help me to let thee love me." Only as we are loved can we really love. When we accept God's love for us in Christ, when we depend upon it, when we receive it into every area of life, then it is that we can love those around us.

"A new commandment I give to you, that you love one another; even as I have loved you."

The future belongs to love because it enriches him who gives it as well as him who receives it. But even more, the future belongs to love because it belongs to God, and God is love. All hatred, falsehood, fear, cruelty, enmity, and bitterness are doomed by love. The resurrection of Christ is the symbol telling us that victory belongs to love, that evil and hatred cannot hold sway over it.

AIDS TO WORSHIP

Hymns: "O Love That Wilt Not Let Me Go"
         "More Love to Thee, O Christ"
Scripture: I Cor. 13

A PRAYER

O God, whose days are without end and whose mercies cannot be numbered, we lift our hearts in thanksgiving to thee. We thank thee for life and the joy of it, for health and all the powers with which thou hast endowed us, for family and friends whose affection and love warms our hearts; and for thy companionship which guides our steps day by day.

Give us radiant spirits assured of thy love and mercy, confident that we cannot move beyond thy fatherly care. Thankful for the life thou hast given us, we ask thee to help us make the most of it. Help us to throw off the shackles of fear and anxiety, of gloom and depression, of pride and prejudice.

In our thanksgiving remind us of our dependence upon others and thee. In our sense of debt to the past give us the incentive to glorify thee in the present, by giving all that we are and have in thy service, through Jesus Christ, our Lord. Amen.

13
Unlock the Doors

In the twenty-sixth verse of the twentieth chapter of John we have these words: "The doors were shut, but Jesus came and stood among them, and said, 'Peace be with you.'"

Here we have the scene of the room in which the disciples were trying to convince doubting Thomas of Christ's triumph over death. They had locked the doors. They did not want to be disturbed. Theirs was an intimate circle, and they wanted the world shut out. But these locked doors could not shut out the Christ. He walked in.

Dr. Ralph W. Sockman says of this scene, "The principles which Christ revealed are as inescapable as the laws of light revealed in the rising sun. The doors of a situation can no more be locked against his laws than they can be locked against the force of gravity."

The point of this story for us today is not merely to refresh our memories with the closed door through which Christ entered into the presence of the disciples, but also to remind ourselves that there are too many doors closed to him today. In too many areas he is shut out. And yet, these doors cannot keep him out. He has a way of coming in.

In the first place, here are our homes. Two young people get married and bind themselves together to establish a home. They are robust in health and full of vigor. A good job insures their financial security. Little children come to bring joy into their lives. The children are given the advantages of excellent schooling, healthy bodies, and good times. How strong seems this family circle! But they shut the doors to religion and the church, feeling no need for them. They are self-sufficient.

Now the question is, How long can they keep their home closed "against the intrusions of issues which Christ raised and the principles he embodied"? Sooner or later he will come in. His truth is so inescapable that homes cannot run long without confronting it.

It may be through the waywardness of a son or daughter that parents will awaken to their need. Then they will know that something has been left out. It may be through the inquiring minds of little children asking questions that are hard to answer. It may be through the invasion of death that unprepared minds through tear-dimmed eyes seek meaning for such sorrow.

But sooner or later the principles of Christ and his truth will have to be dealt with. Locked doors cannot keep him out.

In the second place, too often we lock him out in

political life. To be sure, we call ourselves a Christian nation, but far too often the phrase is a phrase only. We open our congressional sessions with prayer and praise to Christ, but how frequently he is forgotten in subsequent legislation. Public officials in high places take their oath of office with a hand resting upon the ancient Scriptures, but in too many cases fraud and corruption mark their administration.

However, we cannot keep Christ out. He comes in through locked doors. Truth and integrity, good will and justice—these we cannot ignore in government. He comes in with them. Now after two global wars, midway in the bloodiest century of recorded history, thoughtful statesmen are saying, "It is Christ or chaos."

We are coming to see more and more, as Dr. Sockman says,

the utter folly of trying to develop law-abiding citizens within nations while the governments themselves are left lawless. There must be codes of law for international as well as interpersonal action. And into these codes must go the principles of the Prince of Peace, even though his name is not mentioned.

And sometimes, sad to say, we close the door to him in the church. When we think more of our machinery than our message, we close the door to him. When petty jealousy and bickering disrupt the fellowship, then we crowd out the Christ. When we let prejudice and pride take the place of bigness and humility, then we close the door. When we think more of ourselves than we do of others, then we are none of his. When we become satisfied with ourselves and forget to take the gospel to the uttermost parts of the world, then we close the door to Christ. When we become so exclusive that we try to keep people out because of social standing, national heritage, or racial inheritance—then we close the door to him.

But although the door is shut, he comes and stands among us. We cannot keep him out. So let us unlock the doors and remember the words of Jesus when he said, "Seek first his kingdom and his righteousness, and all these things shall be yours as well."

Although we may lock the doors of our homes, our businesses, our political life, to him and his truth; yet the locked doors cannot shut him out, for "without him life becomes stagnant and diseased, bitter and self-destructive."

We must open the doors and give him permanent occupation, that life may be cleansed and purified, redeemed and restored. "The doors were shut, but Jesus came and stood among them, and said, 'Peace be with you!'"

AIDS TO WORSHIP

Hymns: "Thou Hidden Source of Calm Repose"
        "Fight the Good Fight"
Scripture: John 20:19-31

A Prayer

Eternal God, in whom there is no darkness and from whom we find light for life's journey, we thank thee for the communities in which we live and for all institutions that make for better living.

We thank thee for the heritage that is ours; for the dreams and ideals which have been handed down to us; for the faith of our fathers living still.

We thank thee for patriotic men and women who give of themselves in public service, and whose self-interest gives way to public welfare.

Give strength to the arm of law;
give wisdom to those who sit in judgment;
give insight to those who make decisions;
give courage to those who stand for the right;
give concern to those who are governed; and
grant us thy presence for the facing of these days,
    through Jesus Christ, our Lord. Amen.

14
Not How Much but How Faithful

There is an uncompleted hotel in the mountains of western North Carolina. It was planned on a magnificent scale; a road seven miles up a steep mountain was built; the framework was erected to the height of eight stories; fixtures for heating and bathing were carried up; the grounds were terraced and shrubs planted. But for what? Nothing but ruin and disintegration, for it was never completed. No top was put on.

Many a life is like that, only half living. There are all the rich capacities of mind and soul with which we are endowed—unused, silent, unproductive. Have you ever felt that way about some person whom you have met—planned on a grand scale with unlimited possibilities and yet never fulfilling his destiny?

The parable of the talents which Jesus told, as recorded in Matthew 25:14-30, tells us about the use of God's investment in us. You remember how the man who was going into another country gathered his servants and delivered unto them his goods. To one he gave five talents, to another two, and to a third just one. The servant who had received the five used what he had to make five more talents. The one who had received two also doubled his. The servant given the one talent went away and dug in the earth and hid his lord's money. Let us look at this story.

In the first place, it suggests to us that life is loaned to be spent. It is a gift of God. This gift is loaned by God to be used. We did not choose to be born; the gift preceded the choice. We were given life. It is a trust. God has invested in us—given us life. How shall we use that which is given?

We get the clue in answer to our question from what the man in the story expected from his servants. He expected their spending. Life is not to be buried, not to be squandered, not to be preserved, but used, spent.

In the second place, this story represents every man as having some talent. "To one he gave five talents, to another two, to another one, to each according to his ability." This is a statement of the inequality of human endowment. The older we get the more real this truth becomes, when we realize that certain graces and gifts have been planted within us and certain others withheld or denied us.

Against this apparent inequality in human endowment we see two balancing truths; first, that each of us is endowed with some gift, some talent; and second, that we are expected to produce only in accordance with the measure with which it has been meted out to us. The two-talent man has fulfilled his task if he explores to the fullest his two; and the same with the one-talent man; he is not expected to produce what the five-talent man does. George Buttrick said, "Perhaps we should not envy greater capacity; it spells greater responsibility."

Jesus has his own way of computing success. Not how many talents have you earned, but how many in proportion to what you had at first.

In the third place, the one-talent man failed to see that his talent was needed. This is the tragedy of the story. He despised his gift. What a tragedy to see or to feel that God has no need for the one talent! Now this man wasn't bad. He didn't steal his master's money. He just hid it. Surely he felt responsible, and he only buried it for safekeeping.

How many of us are like that! When we are asked to do a job, we often say, "Let someone else do it; they can do it better than I." To be sure, to feel inadequate may be a healthy virtue, but we must never forget that what we have to offer, God can use. Never forget what amazing achievements God has wrought through unlikely instruments, instruments which are placed in his hands. Many have so little to offer and yet give so much. Not what treasure but what faithfulness!

Jesus gave repeated and surprising emphasis to what many called obscure service. He spoke of the importance of the cup of cold water given in love. He insisted that to feed the hungry and to visit the sick was of infinite value. We find emphasized the widow's mite, the unknown Simon carrying the cross, the little boy feeding the five thousand.

Finally, the one-talent man lacked the courage to accept the risk of adventure. This is the crux of the story—"I was afraid." He was afraid, so he buried that which he had been given and thereby lost it. He was afraid of work. He was lazy. He was afraid of his master. He was afraid that he wouldn't be given a fair deal.

The result was that when the master returned he said, "Take the talent from him and give it to him that has the ten." This was not a cruel threat, but a sober fact of life—a true statement of the living law.

Dr. George Buttrick has so well said: "Feed a capacity for music or for sympathy, and it will grow with an ever deeper root. Neglect it and it will disappear. . . . Employ the instinct for prayer. . . and soon the skies will be filled with spiritual hosts. Bury the instinct and soon those selfsame skies will be as inert as slag."

Not how much but how faithful!

AIDS TO WORSHIP

Hymns: "A Charge to Keep I Have"
       "Take Time to Be Holy"
Scripture: Matt. 25:14-30

A Prayer

Our Father, we thank thee for the Christian church and the manifold ways in which she has ministered to life. We are especially grateful for her interest in truth and knowledge. We remind ourselves of the sacred and solemn trust that has led her to spread piety and truth throughout history.

Grant to us all boldness to examine and faith to trust all truth. When we are faced with difficult decisions and are confronted with change beyond our understanding, give to us quiet minds and steady nerves. When we do not know which way to turn or which course to take, restrain us from hasty action and give us the faithfulness of learners and the courage of believers in thee, through Jesus Christ, our Lord. Amen.

15
Where Is the Church?

Emil Brunner reminds us that the New Testament knows nothing of the church as "an institution," but rather as a community of persons related to God and to one another through Christ. He says that we should not say that the church is itself an institution, but only that it has an institution.

Thus, the church is not limited to a physical place, a locality, a physical institution, but rather it is in action wherever God's people are at work. In a rather disturbing and challenging article entitled "The New Biblical Theology in Parish Life," in the journal *Religion in Life*, Dr. Paul van Buren argues that the medieval concept of the parish covering the whole of life has been lost, replaced by a restricted pattern of activity located within a church building. He says that by contrast the gospel is concerned with the world where men and women live and work. This is where the real church is.

"Where is your church?" he asks. Then he answers,

Well, let's see, about this time of the morning, most of it is at work, except for those on the night shift, or those who are sick. Some are at work in this factory and that, others are working in this office or that store, some are in school, some in their kitchen, the Church is infiltrated through the whole town right now. . . . It's spread all through the town involved in all sorts of work, doing that work in such a way and talking in such a way as to let others know what is already true: that Jesus Christ is the boss of this city and all that goes on in it. This is the Church's work. And then, one day a week, we rest from our Church work and gather together to hear again our Lord speaking to us, that we may go back renewed to the task he has set before us.

To be sure, there is a vital place for the expression of our fellowship within the church building and for teaching and worship. All this is vital, but the matter does not end here. This is only part of the church's life, limited within the confines of a building it uses as headquarters, but out where we live is our field of operations. We come here to set our sights, to find strength in our fellowship together, to gain inspiration through worship, to feel anew the presence of Christ in our corporate worship, but out there is where we witness day by day for him.

When Jesus gave us our marching orders sending us into all the world, he meant for us to carry his gospel and its deeper meanings into business, industry, politics, the professions, in our homes, in our play, and in our solitude—yes, into the arena of everyday life. But the church is in all these areas in the persons of its members. The impact upon our world and in all areas of it "is determined far less by what the clergy proclaim on Sunday than by what the laity represent from Monday to Saturday."

Let us then give ourselves with vigor to the institution of the church that it might be strong and virile, but let us always keep in mind that the institution is not an end within itself, but headquarters for great operations for Christ out in the world.

What is the function and task of the church today? William Temple, the late Archbishop of Canterbury, said that

the function of the church is primarily to be itself—the People of God, the Household of the Lord, the Body and Bride of Christ. And that secondarily its function is to win the world unto itself. It is not a means to the Kingdom which can be discarded when the Kingdom is come; rather the coming of the Kingdom is the perfecting of the Church.

He gives us a graphic picture of the function of the church and its nature by calling to mind the figure of a draped lantern.

It is only a lantern at all because the light is in it. Yet, it cannot be a lantern and consist only of the flame which gives the light. The other material of which it is made—the framework and the glass sides—can perfectly serve the lantern's purpose of giving light. But if the glass is faulty and soiled, and if the whole is shrouded with a veil, the light will either be dimmed or else will not reach the outer world at all. So in the Church the true light shines because in it the Gospel is read and the Bread of life is offered. If these be not done, there is no Church at all. But the world which looks on may never see the light because the lives of the members of the Church, including those who read the Gospel and offer Bread, betray the treasure entrusted to them.

AIDS TO WORSHIP

Hymns: "The Church's One Foundation"
"My Hope Is Built on Nothing Less"
Scripture: Eph. 3:14-21

A PRAYER

Eternal God, our dwelling place in all generations, under whose guidance our fathers walked, and by whose strength they were sustained, we pray that the spirit that kindled their faith may descend on us today.

We thank thee for the church and for memories of rich experiences in days gone by, for little children who have given us glimpses of thy nature, for young people who have called us back to dreams of yesterday, for older people who have faced life's sunset years with unwavering hope, and above all for the manifestations of thy presence working among us.

We pray for the church in this perilous time—that she might be a worthy witness of thy truth, that she might call young and old to total commitment to thee, that she might continually find renewal of life at the foot of the Cross, that her mission might be clear, and that all who labor in her ranks might ring true as faithful disciples of thine. In the spirit of Christ we pray. Amen.

16
The Perseverance of God
(*New Year's Day*)

In Isaiah 40:28 we have these words: "Have you not known? Have you not heard? The Lord is the everlasting God, the Creator of the ends of the earth. He does not faint or grow weary."

In this verse we have a suggestion dealing with the perseverance of God. He is an everlasting God, the Lord, the creator of the ends of the earth. He is the God of time and of space. "His eternity stands above the events of time, yet He manifests himself in all the events of history; his creation declares him Lord of the universe, but he gives power to those who have no strength."

Here in this verse the prophet Isaiah is "inspiring persons who are weary and overcome with drudgery and who are shadowed with despair. He is pointing them to the God of yesterday, of today and of tomorrow—to one who is from everlasting to everlasting, God."

How we need to fasten our minds and attention upon the greatness of God! Sidney Lanier in his lovely poem "The Marshes of Glynn" speaks of this in these lines:

As the marsh-hen secretly builds on the watery sod,
Behold I will build me a nest on the greatness of
  God: . . .
By so many roots as the marsh-grass sends in the sod
I will heartily lay me a-hold on the greatness of God.

We want to know that our God is one who never lets up, who never lets down, and who never lets go. Sometimes we feel that he does weary of us and lets us down—especially when trouble comes. But then we remember that he has never promised to save us completely from trouble. To be sure, we may be spared trouble by following him and accepting his way as our way and not bucking his laws, but following him is no insurance policy against it. No one can look at the life of Jesus nor at Paul and believe that. We face trouble, disappointment, sorrow, heartache, and death as Christians.

But God has promised to save us in trouble. His strength enables us to see it through. To the burdened he says: "Come to me, all who labor and are heavy-laden, and I will give you rest." To the fearful he says: "Be not afraid; for behold, I bring you good news of a great joy." To the lonely he says: "Lo, I am with you always, to the close of the age." To the bereaved he says: "Let not your hearts be troubled." To the bored he says: "I came that [you] may have life, and have it abundantly." To us all he says: "My peace I give to you; not as the world gives do I give to you. Let not your hearts be troubled, neither let them be afraid."

This is all to say that he never grants to us any experience unless he also offers strength to see it through. So with Paul we can say, "I can do all things in him who strengthens me."

Then we know he never lets us go. He is unwearied in his search for the souls of men. In Deuteronomy 4:31 we have these words: "For the Eternal . . . will not let you go." (Moffatt) And as Walt Whitman puts it: "Not until the sun excludes you do I exclude you."

Faith then is not merely our holding on to God, but it is also God holding on to us. God is continually in search of each of us and never rests his search. In the verse we have a clue to the relentless search of God for all his children. His perseverence is never willing to let us go.

It means simply this—that God can be trusted. It means that "all things work together for good to them that love him and put their stay in him." In other words, we do believe that the future belongs to God and that we need never be afraid.

Gerald Kennedy puts it like this, "I believe God puts his hand on every life and when we do God's will, all goes well. If I turn my back upon him, all goes wrong. What counts at the end of the day is whether or not we have followed the vision."

It is to give your life into God's hands and know

that he never leaves you alone. You are his. Though you cannot see the way ahead, remember there is purpose and a plan in it. We must trust him and find joy in life.

Every day be grateful for the day that is ahead. Thank God for it. Be faithful to the little tasks at hand and know that the future will be cared for. God has bought you for a price and laid his hand upon you. This I believe.

Sometimes we have to believe this while we are walking through the darkness. We have to remember the light of day. Often it is like driving through a dark tunnel, all the while knowing that at the other end light will appear.

Edward Howard Griggs put it like this: "To be able to stand in the midst of darkness and live as though all about you was light is the final test of the human spirit."

Indeed, we were made to live like this! We soon discover that faith and hope were made for a time of discouragement. Faith isn't faith until it exerts itself in the presence of evil. In spite of all, you know that God is, that this is his world, and that you belong to him. Indeed, the future belongs to God!

AIDS TO WORSHIP

Hymns: "O for a Faith That Will Not Shrink"
        "Lord, for Tomorrow and Its Needs"
Scripture: Isa. 40:1-11; 28-31

A Prayer

Eternal God, our Father, in whose hands our lives rest and in whose world we spend our days, we are grateful for this day's life and for this hour of worship. Help us to push back the curtain of a secular world which would obscure thee, that we may feel thy presence and fasten our minds and hearts upon the reality of thy nature.

Give us a glimpse of thy purpose for life and especially thy purpose for our lives. Help us to know that the very hairs of our heads are numbered, that the pathway we are to tread is lighted by thee. We know that thou dost speak to us, and that we can hear if we are still and listen. What we hear, we are to follow, if life is to be full and free. Give us the will to say "Yes" to the promptings of thy spirit, and the courage to follow thy way. Free us from ill will toward anyone, from pride which fills us with pretense; but fill us with love which knows no barrier and with courage which cannot be shaken. Remind us day by day of our dependence upon thee and help us to amend our lives according to thy holy will, through Jesus Christ, our Lord, we pray. Amen.

17
The Cross Confronts Us Today
(Palm Sunday)

We can think of Christianity without thinking of
churches, creeds, dogmas, ritual, priests, ministers,
but not without the Cross, for it is the central symbol
of our faith.

Listen to the words of this hymn:

> In the cross of Christ I glory,
>   Towering o'er the wrecks of time;
> All the light of sacred story
>   Gathers round its head sublime.
> When the woes of life o'ertake me,
>   Hopes deceive and fears annoy,
> Never shall the cross forsake me:
>   Lo! it glows with peace and joy.

What does the Cross mean to us today?

Stanley Jones has well said that wherever you find
sin and love meeting, you have a cross. These two
words in reality describe the real meaning of the
Cross—sin and love. In the Cross we see sin at its
worst. Here life at its best is confronting life at its
worst. Here is sin in all of its stark reality. The fact of

the Cross is the result of the fact of sin. Nothing but evil in the hearts of men could do this to a man who had done no harm.

Jesus was one who went about doing good—healing the blind, causing the lame to walk, bringing new hope to the fallen, restoring self-respect in the outcast, pointing men to the only way life will work. He was kind, tender, courageous, loving. He asked no favors in return for the good he did except that men should give their lives to God. But cruel and evil men feared the light he brought lest it reveal the darkness of their lives. His goodness threatened their meanness, so they crucified him.

And wherever we find sin today we can find a cross and be reminded of that Cross which crucified our Lord. When we are tempted to take it lightly and try to ignore it by calling it such names as ignorance, unfulfilled good, human error, or mistake, let us turn our eyes to that Cross yonder outside Jerusalem and know that sin always does that to life. It crucifies the best in life. In a real sense it pierces the heart of God. It puts him again upon a cross. When we look upon the Cross, the central symbol of our faith, and see with fresh eyes its victim, a voice from within cries: "That's what your sin means; behold your handiwork!"

Then, we come to that other word suggested by the Cross—love. We see not only the depths of sin but also the heights of love. From despair we move to hope. The Cross lifts into clear relief God's unconquerable love for us. All understanding of the Cross must start with the love of God. "For God so loved the world that he gave his only Son."

It begins with a love which desires to restore the old relationship we have broken through sin or to be lead into a new relationship with the Father into which we have never entered.

The Cross was the only course open for God to use through which his children as free moral agents could understand his love and desires for them. "If it be possible, let this cup pass from me." In other words, if there be any other way—but there wasn't. Now that we have the Cross, we know as never before what love really means. Here was Jesus exhibiting the loving heart of God, suffering because of sin, and longing with intensity that men might be reconciled and return to the Father. Now we know, as we could have never known, that we are important to God, that however humble a place we may hold, God values us and is deeply concerned about us. It tells us that we need never despair, for at the heart of the universe is one who cares.

And it is in this love that we find life's greatest power. The power of the Cross has lifted the world. Jesus said, "And I, if I be lifted up, will draw all men unto me." George Terryl said in these oft-quoted words: "Again and again I have been tempted to give up the struggle, but always the figure of that Strange Man hanging on the Cross sends me back to my task again." When we are "tempted to give up," as we often are, there is no other power like the drawing power of God's love revealed in the Cross that will keep us going and send us back again and again to carry on.

It is a love that goes beyond what is expected. Several years ago a soldier wounded in the South Pacific was sent home to be hospitalized. He is still trying to find the name of the corporal who had saved his life. In a hopeless situation this corporal had crawled and carried him to safety and then disappeared. Who was he? The soldier wants to know and will always want to know. He cannot get away from such a sacrificial act. Neither can you and I.

The reason the Cross touches us today is because we know that it represents the heart of God in forgiving love that would call us home again. It is a love that took it upon itself so that we might know. "God so loved the world!"

AIDS TO WORSHIP

Hymns: "In the Cross of Christ I Glory"
   "Jesus, Keep Me Near the Cross"
Scripture: John 3:1-21

A Prayer

O God, we thank thee for high hours of worship that have led many to see thy face and to call thee Father. Call us back to visions of yesterday. Lure us forward to far horizons of tomorrow. Forbid that we should give thee the leftovers of our strength, the ragged ends of our visions, the fragments of our substance. But grant that we may give the best that we have to the highest that we know, that we may put our utter trust in thee, and that we may never be afraid of the future.

Help us to see with clearer eyes that thy way is the only way, and that it is only in surrender to thee that we gain the joy and freedom that come to those who know and love thee, through Jesus Christ our Lord. Amen.

18

The Risen Christ—A Living Presence

(*Easter*)

Some years ago R. W. Dale, one of England's greatest preachers, was preparing his sermon for Easter when the truth of the Resurrection suddenly seized him. Later he wrote of this experience in his diary. Here is what he wrote:

"Christ is alive," I said to myself: "alive!" And then I paused: "Alive!" And then I paused again: "Alive!" Can that really be true? Living as really as I myself am? I got up and walked about repeating: "Christ is living! Christ is living!" At first it seemed strange and hardly true, but at last it came upon me as a burst of sudden glory; yes, Christ is alive. It was to me a new discovery. I thought that all along I had believed it; but not until that moment did I feel sure about it. I then said, "My people shall know it. I shall preach it again and again until they believe it as I do now."

This is the most important fact in life—that Christ is alive and present in our midst. In the twenty-eighth chapter of Matthew we have recorded how Mary Magdalene and the other Mary went in the early dawn of that first Easter morn to see the tomb. But an angel spoke to them and said, "Do not be afraid; for I know that you seek Jesus who was crucified. He is not here; for he is risen, as he said. Come, see the place where he lay."

Roy L. Smith said that this "solemn declaration, 'He is not here, but is risen,' marked the dividing line between life and death, between hope and hopelessness in human affairs."

In the upper room on that night before the Crucifixion Jesus told his disciples, "I will not leave you desolate; I will come to you. Yet a little while, and the world will see me no more, but you will see me; because I live, you will live also."

It must have been a puzzling statement to those disciples that night. It should have been one that would have brought forth joy, but they did not understand. After the crucifixion they remembered what he had told them. The promise seemed to them fantastic, except for one thing, as Leonard Griffith reminds us—it actually happened. And every year Christians the world over celebrate the festival of Easter, giving praises to God that our Lord's promise was fulfilled.

G. K. Chesterton once wrote: "If a dozen honest men tell me that they have climbed the Matterhorn, I am satisfied that the summit is accessible, though I may never get there myself." But more than a dozen men and women testify that they saw Jesus Christ alive after he had been pronounced dead.

But let us go further and say that Easter marked

not only Christ's resurrection, but it also marked their resurrection. Something happened to these disciples! Leonard Griffith puts it like this:

Something restored their faith and kept it alive in the face of persecution, suffering and martyrdom. Something restored their hope and kept it alive when the world made mockery of their dreams. Something restored their love and kept it alive when all men hated them and called them fools. Something restored their zeal for God's kingdom and kept it alive, until the Church of the Upper Room became the Church of the four corners of the earth. We may doubt the disciples' verbal witness as to what happened on Easter Day, but there is one thing we cannot doubt and that is the witness of their own lives, electric with the resurrection life of Jesus Christ.

"It was not," as someone has said, "the memory of a Galilean Carpenter, but the resurrection of the living Christ which made Jesus the chief regenerative power in the world's history."

On Easter Day we celebrate not only the fact that Christ is alive, that he rose from the dead, and that his living presence quickened the life of these early disciples, but that it happens again today. Easter not only happened; it happens.

The blind George Matheson put it this way: "Son of man, whenever I doubt of life, I think of thee. Nothing is so impossible as that thou shouldest be dead. I can imagine the hills to dissolve in vapor and the stars to melt in smoke, and the rivers to empty themselves in sheer exhaustion: but I feel no limit in thee."

Today, this same spirit is here waiting to touch our lives and put new life into them. The risen Christ is one who turns our sorrows into abiding joy, our fear into courage, routine and dullness into thrilling adventure. He takes a man without a purpose in life and gives him a reason for living, a man without direction and gives him a cause worth dying for.

It is a growing experience. People speak to him, listen to him, consult him, and are guided by him. He calms their fears. He shares their sorrows. He disturbs them in their complacency. He is their hope, their strength, their purpose, their very reason for living. In him indeed is the Resurrection made real.

Easter happened; it happens; and may it happen in you today!

"I will not leave you desolate; I will come to you. Yet a little while, and the world will see me no more, but you will see me, because I live, you will live also."

AIDS TO WORSHIP

Hymns: "Christ the Lord Is Risen Today"
       "Crown Him with Many Crowns"
Scripture: Matt. 28

A Prayer

O God, our Father, whose love has never let us go and beyond whose care we cannot drift, once more we lift our hearts to thee. We would quiet our souls in thy presence and rest ourselves in the confidence of thy sustaining strength.

We come before thee this day unworthy of thy love; we come stained by temptations which so easily beset us. We come feeling need of thee, thy power, thy strength, thy forgiveness. Thou knowest us better than we know ourselves. Take us this day and lift us upward. Strengthen our steps, enlarge our visions, quicken our hopes, purify our motives. Remind us of the things which do not change, and secure us to life's unfading treasures, through Jesus Christ, our Lord. Amen.

19
To Live in the Afterglow of Easter
(*Post-Easter*)

To live in the afterglow of Easter is to see and have faith in the good news of the gospel, as James S. Stewart put it, "that God has invaded history with power and great glory; that Christ is alive now and present through his spirit; that through the risen Christ there has been let loose into the world a force which can transform life beyond recognition."

Certainly to live in the afterglow of Easter demands a new outlook on life—a "stretching and strengthening of the soul." Paul is speaking of this when he writes to the Christians at Philippi: "Have this mind among yourselves, which you have in Christ Jesus." He is saying, Look at life through Christ's eyes.

Indeed, the joy of living is determined not so much by what life brings to us as by the attitude we bring to life, not so much by what happens to us as by the way we look at what has happened. Our living is determined more by our attitudes than by our ancestors. Great living comes with great outlooks. What life does to us depends on what life finds in us. And what life finds in us is dependent on our outlooks, our attitudes, our motives. Victorious living has to do with outlook. Christianity is a way of looking at life through the eyes of Christ.

We are reminded that any view of life has four dimensions—height, depth, breadth, length. Living in the afterglow of Easter does something to each dimension.

In the first place, we gain a new height to the idea of God. Paul expresses this when he wrote in Philippians 2:9-11 these majestic words: "Therefore God has highly exalted him and bestowed on him the name which is above every name, that at the name of Jesus every knee should bow . . . and every tongue confess that Jesus Christ is Lord, to the glory of God the Father."

Paul is here saying that at the heart of life is a loving God, whose suffering love for all men was expressed through Jesus Christ, our Lord, and that before such love men can do no other than bow the knee and confess that he is Lord to the glory of God the Father. It is a name which is above every name, a new name which by way of his humiliation he has won as universal Lord. Three times in his epistles Paul quotes this formula: "Jesus is Lord."

In this new height to an understanding of God we know that it is this love that will win the world. It is this love which is at the heart of life. It is this love from which we cannot escape and which will not let us go. No other power can save man from himself and yet leave at the same time his freedom.

In the second place, living in the afterglow of Easter brings a new depth to life. The spirit and mind of Christ go beyond the form to the heart of life, beyond externals to the center of life. He is concerned more with the inside of the dish than the outside. He warns men to be more careful about what proceeds out of the mouth than about what goes into it. For him motive takes precedence over all outward acts and deeds. Through his eyes man is judged not so much by what he has as by what he is.

In the third place, living in the afterglow of Easter brings a new breadth to life by the inclusive love of Jesus. We build walls and fences; Jesus breaks them down. We exclude; he includes.

With this new breadth which Jesus gives comes a genuine sense of tolerance for the failures and faults of other people. Arrogance and pride give way through his eyes to humility and understanding. In our own failures we learn to be kind in attitude to the failures of others. The Cross and its attendant evils, and his sacrificial love made known through it, humble us. In the glow of such love we confess that he is Lord and all men are his children, that all men belong to the family of God.

Finally, there is a new length to our outlook as Jesus brings us into the presence of eternity. In him we find time and eternity meeting. We think in terms of small blocks of time—days, weeks, months, years; but God thinks in terms of eternity. The psalmist said, "A thousand years in thy sight are but as yesterday."

Now, living on this side of Easter, we know that we are not riding a local but a through train. We are but pilgrims in this earth, and here we have no continuing city. Our true citizenship is in heaven. What it means to us to see life not merely in terms of time but eternity! And it is Christ who makes us know that we are somebody going somewhere, that life has a destiny, and that that destiny belongs to God.

AIDS TO WORSHIP

Hymns: "O For a Thousand Tongues to Sing"
"Lead On, O King Eternal"
Scripture: Phil. 2:1-11

A Prayer

Eternal God, Father of all mercies and God of all comfort, we lift our hearts and voices to thee this day in grateful praise.

We thank thee for saints and prophets whose vision of the Eternal has lighted our paths and strengthened our hearts. We praise thy name for all valiant souls who, facing adversity and hardships, still believed in thy goodness and whose faith has strengthened our faith.

Especially are we thankful for the wonder and majesty of thy nature as we know thee in Christ and for thy love which will not let us go and which cannot be altered by life's changing moods. We thank thee that thou art near us even when we are unaware of thy presence, and that thy purposes for us are always merciful and good.

Forgive us for whimpering and whining when we should be grateful. Free us from the perils of pride. Keep us humble of heart, knowing that thou dost give us more than we deserve.

Give us grace, we beseech thee, to show forth thy praise not only with our lips but in our lives, committing ourselves wholly to thy service. In the name of Christ we pray. Amen.

20
The Church in Thy House
(*Christian Family Week*)

In the sixteenth chapter of Paul's letter to the
Romans we find these words, "Greet Prisca and
Aquila, my fellow-workers in Christ Jesus, who risked
their necks for my life; . . . greet also the church in
their house."

The New Testament church was in a house before
it was in a church building. Over and over again
Jesus preached in a house. And toward the latter
days of his earthly ministry, he told his disciples
to go to a certain place and tell the owner that he
wanted to use a room in his home—the "upper
room." We find him teaching and preaching in a
room in a certain house, when, because of the crowd,
all could not get in. So the man who was ill was let
down on his bed through the roof that he could
be in the presence of Jesus. It was to the home of
Mary and Martha that Jesus frequently went; and
there was the church.

Let us look at the church in thy house.

In the first place, the church in thy house must
have a faith that is vital. God must be in the center.
There must be a seeking after and a following of his
will. He must be a welcome guest.

It is said that one morning Martin Luther went down to breakfast and found his wife dressed in black. He said, "Dear, why are you dressed in black?" She answered, "God is dead!" "What do you mean? God is not dead." "Well," she responded, "you are acting as if he were dead."

Then there is the Bible. It should not be an ornament on the living room table. It must be an open book. Some years ago Leslie Howard, from a camp in France, sent a copy of the New Testament to his godchild. On the flyleaf of the book he wrote these words, "Get your father to read often to you from this book. So many people seem to have forgotten it."

Then there must be prayer. These go together. I don't know how many of us pray in our homes, but no church can be vital unless there are praying fathers, mothers, and children. Dr. George Buttrick has said that "prayer is the lost word of this generation and must be found again."

In the second place, the church in thy house must not only have a faith, but must be a miniature Christian community. Its members must not only read the Bible, talk about God, offer heartfelt prayers, but there must be in actual practice those things which are believed.

Praying for forgiveness is not very real unless father forgives. Talking about God means little unless we live as if he is. Memorizing "Do unto others as you would have them do unto you" has little significance unless kindliness is shown to all the family. As parents we should get together and make our homes miniature Christian communities.

Children know if we really value the church and love God. They know that there is something shallow in our faith if we give God only the scraps from our tables—in time, in financial support, in dedicated service. If we give more to the club than to the church, something is wrong with our values, and our children will know it. If we consistently neglect to attend God's service, it is giving eloquent testimony that God doesn't matter and that we are not recommending him to our children. If we are extremely critical of the church, our children will know that we really don't love it. Eloquent testimony! If we are members of the official family of the church and seldom attend its meetings, what better way can we have of telling our family and the world that it really doesn't make much difference?

What greater memory or legacy could we leave our children than the memory of a Christian home, a miniature Christian community?

Finally, the church in thy house must have the strength which comes from the church in God's house. They must work hand in hand. It is not enough just to have a Christian home in a community, for to have such a home you need the church in God's house. The church in your house can never be vital unless there is an active participation in God's house.

Roy L. Smith tells the story about a well-groomed

lady who came into the preacher's study one morning and told him that she would like for him to help her with her son. The minister was very interested and took a pad and pencil, and asked her the boy's age, name, address, and asked her if she and her husband came to his church. The mother answered, "No, but we do live in the neighborhood, and my son knows some of the boys in your church school."

The minister then told her that during the next week he would have one of the men from the men's class call on her husband at his office and one of the ladies from the mother's class call on her. Then he said, "I will meet all three of you here at the church school next Sunday."

"Oh, no, I only wanted to see you about my son. He needs the church school."

The minister became very serious and said, "Yes, my good lady, I, too, would like to see someone get your boy into church school. But if anyone is to get him in, you and your husband are the ones who are going to have to do it."

The church in your house will not be real unless there is a direct link between your house and God's house.

AIDS TO WORSHIP

Hymns: "Happy the Home When God Is There"
   "Love Divine, All Loves Excelling"
Scripture: Rom. 16:1-5

A PRAYER

Dear God, who art the Father of us all and who hast established the homes of our world, we thank thee that in our homes we can find thee. Grant that the love we have for one another may be strengthened by the love we have for thee. Bless us, we pray, in all our family relationships.

Help us to make room for thy presence in our midst to the end that Christ may be the Lord of our homes. In his name we pray. Amen.

21
Christianity Began with a Gift
(*Stewardship Sunday*)

Every church considers at least once a year how much it will provide for its program in the way of a budget. Of course we cannot evaluate what the church means to us merely in material terms and by what we can afford to give to it, but we do know that our gifts for the support of its work are a tangible way in which we do measure our affection or indifference to the church.

Some may feel that the church is always asking for money for some cause or another, and it is well to remind ourselves that the church will always be asking for money—that is, as long as it is the church of Jesus Christ. Why is this so?

It is because Christianity began with a gift. It was the gift of God to mankind in the form of a Son who is the Savior of the world. It was the gift of God that came out of his great heart of love to all men. Every Christmas we are reminded of that gift which is ours for the acceptance and which brings with it gladness of heart. "Behold, I bring you good news of a great joy which will come to all the people;

112

for to you is born this day in the city of David a Savior, who is Christ the Lord." Indeed, it is life's supreme gift!

Again, in John 3:16 we are reminded of this gift: "For God so loved the world that he gave his only Son, that whoever believes in him should not perish but have eternal life."

So from the very first, giving is involved in our faith. Love—the love of God—prompted that first gift to mankind, and for us who embrace the faith love prompts us to give. Real love goes beyond feeling to action. It is always giving and giving. Jesus knew that this principle of action is the most characteristic trait of real love. He was forever urging people to act. "This do in remembrance of me." "Go and do thou likewise." Look at him picture the relationship of love to action in the good Samaritan! To be sure the priest and Levite "felt sorry" for the wounded wayfarer, but not sorry enough. They refused to help actively. Their love wasn't deep nor vital. So they "passed by on the other side." But love never passes by on the other side.

And it is because of what God has done for us that out of grateful hearts we are moved to give. It happens every time when we are confronted with the love of God through Christ.

In the second place, the church of Jesus Christ will always be asking for money because of our need to give. Jesus knew that nothing determines character more than the way we make and the way we spend

113

our money. And yet he never spoke of money as an evil within itself, or as useless. He said that the test was what men do with it, and what it does to them.

Jesus saw that nothing determines character so much as the way we make and the way we use money. We often say, "Money talks!" Indeed it does, for if you get to know two things about an individual, you will have real clues to his character—how he makes and how he spends his money. Nothing throws a searchlight into a man's soul as does this test.

Now let us turn to these words found in Luke 12:34, where Jesus utters a very searching and penetrating truth: "Where your treasure is, there will your heart be also." Surely he would have us ask some questions about our treasure. Where is my treasure? What do I care for most? What gains my first allegiance? What do I consider of supreme importance?

Jesus is saying that our hearts lie where our desire, or treasure, lies. In other words, our interests in life soon capture our hearts. We become like that after which we seek. It was Marcus Aurelius who put it this way: "Every man is worth just as much as the things are worth about which he is concerned."

In the third place, the church will always be asking for money because it costs to operate a church. And it costs to belong to the church, and it always will.

It cost in the days of old. It cost the widow her mite. For the sake of the church Stephen was stoned to death. That it might spread and grow, Paul gave all that he had, finally his life. Judson went to Burma,

Grenfell to Labrador, and Schweitzer to Africa—all for the sake of the church.

There are underground tunnels outside the city of Rome, called catacombs, where members of the early church used to assemble for worship and to bury their dead. They found shelter in caves to escape persecution because of their membership in the church. They knew something about the high cost of being a Christian.

The church continues to cost today. We could recount incident after incident of heroic service to the church in far-off places which cost and cost dearly many stalwart Christians.

Finally, when we care deeply, we give joyously. When we give joyously, it comes out of a heart of love. We give spontaneously. It does not have to be prompted. It is not done out of duty but out of deep feeling.

You remember the beautiful story of the woman who broke the alabaster box over the feet of Jesus. It was done impulsively. It was out of the overflow of deep feeling and appreciation. When she broke that box and poured it over the head and feet of the Savior, it was not a calculated act. It was not done because it was the right thing to do nor because it was her duty to do it. But rather it was done with a gay, reckless abandonment. She did not have to spur herself onward or tell herself that she would gain merit in the eyes of the Master if she did it. No, it came out of a heart that felt deeply, out of a soul that was filled with devotion.

This is the kind of giving that Jesus commends. Giving that is joyous and glad. Giving that is freely done. It is the kind that brings joy to the giver.

AIDS TO WORSHIP

Hymns: "Lord, Speak to Me"
       "Awake, Awake to Love and Work"
Scripture: Matt. 6:19-33

A Prayer

Once again, our Father, we pause to lift our hearts in gratitude to thee for this thy gift to mankind. Our minds are too small to grasp the significance of this gift; we know that here is more than we can comprehend.

We do believe that thou hast acted in history in this divine event by coming into the world in a form that we can better understand. But the wonder of it, the simplicity of it, the majesty of it—this is more than we can fathom.

But we are grateful, O God, to know that it is not for us to fully understand, but to accept this event as a measure of thy love and compassion for sinful humanity. Help us, we pray, to respond to thy love by giving ourselves anew to thee.

Help us to be still, to wait in silence, to throttle our fevered rush—so that thou canst speak to us thy word of peace and joy. In Christ's name we pray. Amen.

22
Soils of Life
(*Rural Life Sunday*)

Jesus was greatly concerned over the soil of human life. We find in the parable of the sower, which should be called the parable of the soils, Jesus saying that numerous seeds of truth are being planted but only a few in good soil. For him the most important thing is not the sower nor the seed, but the soil into which seeds are sown. He came to sow truth into the lives and hearts of men, but in only a few do they take root.

Here we find the Master seated in a boat on the shore of the Sea of Galilee. "And there were gathered unto him great multitudes"—they were the soil. Just why had they come? Dr. George Buttrick lists several reasons. Some came out of curiosity—to see what this talked-of man was like. Some came from self-seeking motives—it might be profitable to be seen in such company. Some came in quick enthusiasm and others in deep yearning for something which would uphold them. Some came as revolutionaries—to make him king, to use him as a party leader.

Just how would they receive his words? The reception would be as varied as the soil of the Galilean hillside is in receiving seed. How often had he seen the sower plant in vain in soil which would not respond. Yes, he would tell them a story about themselves—how his words would be received and why some would find no lodgment in them.

Jesus knew that in many it would take no root and that they, like men today, would be quick to blame the sower or the seed and slow to blame the soil— to blame themselves.

"And he told them many things . . . saying, 'A sower went out to sow. And as he sowed, some seeds fell along the path, and the birds came and devoured them.' Here it found no lodgment. The wind blew it away. Birds came and gathered at will.

Here we have the hard life. The life which had the same soil as others, but had it trampled. They had made their souls a thoroughfare. The path had not always been hard. Once it was mellow like the rest of the field, but it has been trodden hard by much travel.

Just what could Jesus do with these men? Certainly nothing at the moment. Something had to stab them awake, had to plow deep into their soil. His truth could not compete with the ways of the world. Perhaps it was pain, trouble, misery which must first break the ground.

"Other seeds fell on rocky ground, where they had not much soil, and immediately they sprang up, since they had no depth of soil, but when the sun rose, they were scorched; and since they had no root they withered away." Here was the shallow ground with a ledge of rock two or three inches below the surface. The harvest on such ground followed the rule of "quickly come, quickly go." Here was the feverish growth which withers from lack of moisture. The sun was too much for the fruit.

How startlingly true this is when applied to human nature. You recall how one would-be disciple said, "I will follow you wherever you go," but Jesus quenched his thin enthusiasm by saying, "Foxes have holes, and birds of the air have nests; but the Son of man has nowhere to lay his head." This man had not counted the cost, and agreed with shallow loyalty.

"Other seeds fell upon thorns, and the thorns grew up and choked them." The ground may be good soil with latent possibilities, but the seed is choked with thorns and dies. Here we have the crowded life—the life that allows the cares of the world and perhaps the eager pursuit of riches or popularity to crowd God's truth from its mind and heart. Here is the person with divided loyalties. His life becomes scattered.

Of course, "thorns" stand for any kind of weed that chokes out the desired crop. Corn is a weed if it grows in a wheatfield. The blackberry is a troublesome thorn if it grows in a flower bed. So even the most innocent occupations and praiseworthy actions may become harmful if allowed to crowd vital truth from our lives. We have just so much time to live and just so much strength to do it with that we must choose.

But, finally, there is good soil. And Jesus said, "Other seeds fell on good soil and brought forth grain, some a hundredfold, some sixty, some thirty." (Matt. 13:8.) So Jesus sowed with hope. For there were in the multitude those who were sin-sick and world-weary, and who came seeking help. The seed sank deep into this soil and took root. Neither the birds, nor sun, nor cares could ruin this harvest, for it was grounded on faith in God.

These valiant spirits gave him hope and cheer, for having heard, they held fast. They are the ones who take time to live. They love little children and take time to enjoy the finer things in life. They are sinners, too, and do make mistakes, but they are always striving for the highest. As Dr. George Buttrick says, "They walk in the light while it is day, and when night comes keep faith with the illumined hour, nor allow the world's glare to make them disobedient."

But let us realize that the soil of life is not in every respect like the soil of nature. Some soils in nature are never usable. The arctic ice fields and sand of the desert yield no food. But human soil is never completely without promise. The soil of the hard life may be cultivated into that of the good. The shallow may be deepened and the crowded may be weeded. Jesus' words can find lodgment in every life, but we must do the cultivating.

AIDS TO WORSHIP

Hymns: "I Would Be True"
       "Lord, Speak to Me"
Scripture: Luke 8:4-15

A Prayer

Almighty God, who hast given us this good land for our heritage, who hast provided for us all the good things of life, forgive us for our failure to share with all men what thou doth provide.

We have made use of the resources of thy earth, have tilled the soil, hewn the forest, and produced in plenty the necessities of this life. The mind of man has mastered the machine and with it filled his barns and storehouses to overflowing. Yet, our Father, some of thy children are crying today for bread which has been burned, clothes which have been stored, fruit which has decayed, and meat which has spoiled.

We have made use of thy bounty in production but have defied thy laws of distribution. Grant us wisdom and the will needed to make these adjustments. Empower us with love which will not rest until it is done. Give us concern, O Lord, for all thy children, who are our brothers. In the spirit of Christ we pray. Amen.

23
Overcoming the Perils of Routine
(*Labor Day*)

There has never been in history a time when mankind was caught more in the routine of life than today. In spite of modern conveniences and timesavers it seems that more than ever we are servants of gadgets. The operation of machines can become a dulling, daily grind which can, if men let it, bring the perils of routine. It can take from life its sense of freshness and rob it of zest. It can add to its own measure of boredom and even rob men of an awareness of God. Trudging through a daily routine with its modern tempo can make it difficult to keep aware of the inspiring Spirit of God.

The necessity, however, of facing the routine of life is not new. In the fourth chapter of John, the fourth verse, we have these words referring to Jesus, "He had to pass through Samaria." Now Samaria was a district which geographically lay between Judea and Galilee and one in which Jesus had no special interest. It was the home of a mixed race formed by a group of imported colonists who intermarried in the land when most of the ten tribes were carried away into captivity.

When the ten tribes returned from captivity, open bitterness broke out between the Jews and Samaritans, so that the Samaritans erected on Mt. Gerizim a temple of their own to Jehovah. Thus, Samaria was not regarded by the Jews as belonging to the Holy Land, but as a strip of foreign country. In New Testament times it was not a separate province, but a part of Judea, possessing no definite boundary lines, but simply a group of cities and towns occupied by these people.

Jesus had no special interest in this district, but still we read, "He had to pass through Samaria." Thus, Samaria might well stand for routine, through which we must pass. And we notice that in this routine journey Jesus found some wells from which he quenched his thirst. Let us look at them.

Here was the historic well of Jacob which is the symbol of refreshment in the midst of the wearying stretches. It was at this well that Jesus met the Samaritan woman. He was on his way to Galilee, and he and his disciples arrived at the city of Samaria tired and dusty from the trip. He stopped to rest at the well thought to have been dug by Jacob.

As he was sitting a woman approached for water. She was a Samaritan. Jesus was alone with her, as the disciples were in the city buying food. He said to her, "Give me a drink."

Of course, this woman was startled when this strange Jew asked her for water. She said, "How is it that you, a Jew, ask a drink of me, a woman of

Samaria?" For Jews have no dealings with Samaritans. Jesus tells her that he can give her "living water." This puzzles the woman, for she sees no bucket. She asks, "Are you greater than our father Jacob, who gave us the well?" Then Jesus answers by saying, "Every one who drinks of this water will thirst again, but whoever drinks of the water that I shall give him will never thirst; the water that I shall give him will become in him a spring of water welling up to eternal life."

Someone has said that "the result of this noonday conversation is that the woman carried the same old waterpot from the same old well over the same hot path to the same little village, but with a new spirit." Under the burden there were new hope and new visions. No longer was the carrying of her waterpots a drudgery. The drudgery and dull routine had changed into new adventure. Now, this happened with Jesus in a place of routine when he must needs go through Samaria. It furnished for him an occasion of opening up living water to this weary and confused woman.

And again it was along this route of routine that the origin of the good Samaritan parable must have come to him, even though he must have been unaware of it. It was out of his trip through Samaria with all its dullness, where he really had no business, that this wonderful parable found its birth.

This all tells us that when we are caught in life's routine there will be similar wells to make us know that God works in life's apparent routine as well as in moments of interesting occupation. We need to see meaning to routine. It may be that there will be creative moments when we least expect them.

The fact is so much of life is spent in the process of life, in the dull necessity of daily tasks, in traveling toward our goals, in seeking the end of our endeavors. And if life is to be satisfying, then there is need for us to see meaning even in its process, and not merely joy when we come to the end of the way. It is to find more than the routine of a journey through Samaria, but to see along the way wells which can quench our thirst. The Spirit of God is at work even in our prosaic labors. Remember this when we travel through our Samarias.

AIDS TO WORSHIP

Hymns: "All Hail the Power of Jesus' Name"
    "Fairest Lord Jesus"
Scripture: John 4:1-14

A Prayer

Eternal God, who hast called us into life and in whose hands our lives do rest, we offer to thee this day our praise and adoration. We come before thee asking that thou would push back the curtain of the spiritual world that we might get a glimpse of thee.

For all sorts and conditions of men we pray:
 for those who are sick in body and disturbed in mind;
 for those burdened with the guilt of sin;

125

for those living under oppression and know not freedom;

for all who labor on farms that men might eat;

for all who patrol streets and fight fires that men might
be safe;

for all who serve their country that it might remain
free;

for all who labor as missionaries that men might hear
the good news;

for all these, O God, we raise our petitions today.

Now we wait before thee, asking that Christ in all
his courage, his steadfastness, his faith, his sympathy,
his victorious power, may reach out to uphold us and
to dwell within us. In his name we pray. Amen.

24
Gazing on Greatness
(World Communion Sunday)

We become like that upon which we habitually gaze. The power of eyes is a force in life which must be reckoned with. All that we see affects us—the billboards along the highway, the movies on the screens, the photographs and pictures in the books and magazines we read. All these things fasten themselves upon us as they impress themselves upon our minds and hearts.

Jesus knew the power of eyes—eyes that see life's physical dimensions and eyes that see the invisible, the eyes of the soul. He knew our need to see frequently the highest and best, to fasten our thoughts and inner vision upon life's most momentous event— the Crucifixion and Resurrection.

And so in the same night that he was betrayed, he took bread;

and when He had given thanks, He brake it, and gave it to His disciples, saying, Take, eat; this is My body, which is given for you; do this in remembrance of Me. Likewise after supper He took the cup and when He had given thanks, He gave it to them, saying, Drink ye all of this, for this is My blood of the new covenant which is shed for you, and for many, for the remission of sins; do this, as oft as ye shall drink it, in remembrance of Me.

What then happens to us when we gaze upon Christ? *We expose ourselves to transforming powers.* With our inner eye we see him in all of his beauty, truth, and bravery so that it writes a message upon our minds and hearts. When we gaze devotedly upon him, we are captured by him. When we become possessed by his divine daring and ardent affection, we submit ourselves to powers that can make new creatures of us. Paul spoke of this when he said, "Do not be conformed to this world, but be transformed." "If any one is in Christ, he is a new creation."

To expose ourselves to Christ's environment is to really worship, and such exposure transforms. We catch something from him that makes us over. We look at his gentleness and kindness, and it becomes part of us. We reflect upon his courage and bravery; we see his deep love for people; we see his sufferings; we share in our thoughts his dreams for mankind; and lo, something happens to us.

There is mystery here. We say of Paul that he was Christlike. How did he get that way? By simply fixing his gaze upon Christ, by giving himself to what he saw, by becoming possessed by Christ in such a way that he could say, "It is no longer I who live, but Christ who lives in me."

Thomas Aquinas and Bonaventure were two of the

wisest men of the thirteenth century. Aquinas was a Dominican monk, famous for both his learning and his piety. Bonaventure was the chief intellectual leader of the Franciscan order. A legend states that once the two spent the day together in learned conversation. Before leaving, Aquinas asked to see Bonaventure's library. He was led to a monastery cell, and opening the door Bonaventure pointed to the crucifix before which he daily prayed. Quietly he said, "There it is."

Power comes when one reverently looks upon Christ and his cross. It is transforming power.

Again, to look upon Christ as we come to Holy Communion stirs us to a need of inward housecleaning. Within us all there are areas which need sweeping and dusting. So, looking upon Christ, seeing his purity, watching his unselfishness, witnessing his bravery, contemplating his holiness—all these make us feel the sense of need within. We see the dirt in our own lives as an enemy of spiritual health.

When we expose ourselves to the light of Christ, what will be uncovered no one can say for another. But many of us are spiritually diseased by hurt feelings that still are festering. Against his life we see unforgiveness. Motives that are evil still lurk in our hearts. Pride and selfishness hold sway in our deeds. Gazing upon him, we cry with the psalmist, "Create in me a clean heart, O God; and put a new and right spirit within me."

What a contrast between his light and our darkness, between his purity and our sordid selves, between his holiness and our evil ways. And yet, as Angus Dun has said, "In him there is offered to us a companionship that cleanses and lifts us up. He humbles us without discouragement. He makes us proud of being men, without conceit. He asks and will take no pretense from us. He shares with us his own large and generous purposes."

We are told that the face of Theresa shone with beauty and charming gladness. It came from her long contemplation of God. It explains how she built many religious houses and how her radiant spirit and works have commanded the attention of the religious world for four hundred years. That power was the result of her gaze upon the Christ.

Here, then, is one meaning of Holy Communion in all of its transforming power. It is relevant to what Paul had in mind when he said, "Whatever is true ... honorable ... just ... pure ... lovely ... worthy of praise ... think [or look with your mind, gaze] about these things."

AIDS TO WORSHIP

Hymns: "Break Thou the Bread of Life"
       "The Church's One Foundation"
Scripture: Luke 22:1-20

A Prayer

Our Father, from the rush and hurry of our busy days we pause to acknowledge thee as Lord of Life. Grant us grace to be quiet in this noisy world, so we may wait for thee.

We come with grateful hearts made glad by this hour of worship. Lift us out of ourselves as we gaze upon thy matchless beauty. Fasten our minds upon timeless truth. Fix our wills on right living and secure our loyalty to thy kingdom.

We thank thee for the light of the knowledge of thy glory that we have seen in the face of Jesus Christ. We thank thee for his coming to redeem us, for his life and teaching, for his tragedy and triumph. He is the way and the truth and the life. O God, make that not only our belief, but our conviction and our experience.

In the name and spirit of Christ we pray. Amen.

25
We Can Make Room
(Advent)

In the second chapter of Luke, the seventh verse, we have these words: "And she gave birth to her first-born son and wrapped him in swaddling cloths, and laid him in a manger, because there was no place for them in the inn."

This is a familiar passage to us all—how crowded conditions in Bethlehem forced Joseph to take his wife Mary to a stable where she was to give birth to her firstborn son. We can imagine the great sense of concern which must have been Joseph's and the anxiety of Mary in being crowded into this tiny stable.

There is an old story about the keeper of the inn, who owned the stable. He had just given rooms to Marcus Riblius, a great man of Rome, with his servants, his scribes, and his guards, and they had filled the place. It kept the old innkeeper rushing to and fro trying to answer the demands of all the things asked of him. Then there were more travelers who came asking that they might abide there for the night.

Then the next morning came one whom the innkeeper would not have turned away for all the silver in the world, if he had only known who he was. In the party were two people—a man who might have been a carpenter or a potter and his wife who was ill. The man asked for room, explaining that his wife could travel no longer because she was ill. The harassed innkeeper grew angry at his pleas and shouted at him saying, "Can I make more rooms arise by striking my staff upon the ground?"

This is another day. This is A.D. and not B.C. So when we close our hearts to him and go our willful, sinful way, we can only say, "I did know better. I did know better." "If only I had accepted the things which belong unto my peace." We have heard those matchless words, "For God so loved the world that he gave his only Son, that whoever believes in him should not perish but have eternal life."

If we crowd him out with our own selfish ways, we do not even have the excuse that the innkeeper had, for we have heard, we have known.

But it is never too late. So let us this Christmas ask ourselves if we are guilty of giving him no room in the inns of our hearts.

For one thing, let us ask ourselves if we have crowded him out in our thoughts. Unless we keep his truths uppermost in our minds, unless we contemplate his matchless wisdom, unless we frequently read from his Book—we crowd him out of our thoughts. But when we think of the Christ of Christmas and let his wisdom take control of our lives, then it is we maintain a sense of the divine at the heart of life and make room for him.

The innkeeper missed the greatest opportunity of his life and the greatest ever had by any innkeeper. Many years afterward it did no good to repeat over and over again, "They were but poor folk, and how was I to know?" When the Christ child was born in the stable and a brilliant light filled the heavens, the great man from Rome, Marcus Riblius, and his servants were still in a drunken sleep, and the innkeeper had missed his greatest chance.

But who are we to be too hard on the innkeeper? Had he only known, had he only known—he would not have missed his chance. He really had no room and was tired and worn by the crowds housed in his inn. He gave the couple what space he had—that in a stable.

But this is another day, and for us there should be another way. For Christ has come and Christmas is real. As the innkeeper could not have known, we now know that Christ is the Son of God. God has spoken in Christ. He has made himself known in a form that we can understand. The Word has become flesh. God has revealed himself supremely. This we have been told.

Again, let us ask ourselves if we have crowded him out of our desires. Jesus said, "Seek ye first the kingdom of God and his righteousness, and all these things shall be added unto you." But too many times we try to live by bread alone and make no room for the Christ of the spirit.

Christ should come first in our lives, and not last. He must be more than an accessory to be given a brief hour on Sunday and then forgotten; we must make room for him in our hearts; we must give him permanent occupation. His way must become paramount. His desire must take precedence. His will must control. We yearn for peace, but peace will come only when the dominant desire the world over becomes Christian.

This Christmas we are reminded that this divine love can be born again in our hearts and homes, that we can open the doors of our hearts to him, that we can make room in the inns of our lives for his spirit.

AIDS TO WORSHIP

Hymns: "O Come, All Ye Faithful"
       "There's a Song in the Air"
Scripture: Luke 2:1-7

A Prayer

Eternal God, in whom our fathers trusted and in whom we trust, thou who hast caused the light of eternal life to shine upon the world; quicken in us, we beseech thee, the sense of thy gracious presence here this day.

As we enter this holy season, help us to think more of the Christ of Christmas than of the cost of Christmas, more of what we are to give than what we are to receive. But whatever we receive this year, help us to receive it with gratitude, and whatever we give, help us to give with cheer.

Help us to be content to keep up with Christ rather than with the crowd. Give us joy in simple things, and grant that whatever we give may be an expression of joy that is in our hearts over the coming of Christ and our desire to share that joy with someone else.

Bless us as we gather around our firesides and as our love is made to glow with thy love in our hearts. Comfort those who mourn and suffer this Christmas, and may they find in thee one who heals our wounds and shares our cares.

Grant that we may make room for Christ in the inns of our hearts and offer ourselves in his service. In Christ's name we pray. Amen.

26
Christmas Overshadows Petty Things
(*Christmas*)

The most familiar passage of scripture relating to Christmas is found in the second chapter of Luke beginning in the eighth verse with these words: "And in that region there were shepherds out in the field, keeping watch over their flock by night." Then we read of the angel announcing the coming of the Lord, born in the city of David. When he had gone away the shepherds said one to another: "Let us go over to Bethlehem and see this thing that has happened, which the Lord has made known to us."

And so with haste they came, for it was the most important thing in their lives at that time. That event served to crowd out the petty things of life; it overshadowed the little events of daily living; it became for them their major concern.

As we move through these days that lead to Christmas, as we once again journey toward Bethlehem, if we are to catch its true significance, it should be for us an experience in which the petty things of life are crowded out by the big things.

In the first place, it is a time to keep spites and animosities from crowding out friendship and love.

137

At Christmastime our loved ones and friends are re-valued as we express our affection in gifts and words. When we make out our lists of remembrances, we add those who for one reason or another have been estranged from us. Christmas helps us forget the little differences and spites that mar relationships with others.

It has a cleansing power about it, if its spirit really takes hold. For one cannot hate and pout in the presence of God's love in Christ. When we witness a love so amazing, so divine—a love which came down at Christmastime—our petty peeves cannot linger in its light.

The magic of the great message of Christmas is that with the coming of the Christ child there came a love into the world which can transform our hatreds and ill will into kindness and forgiveness. In the face of such forgiving love, one cannot hate.

Christmas comes and with it a cleansing power. Enemies are tempted to forget their differences, and estranged friends are brought together. What a Christmas it will be if the love of God through Christ floods your soul and drives out hatred and bitterness and cynicism!

In the second place, Christmas is a time to keep little annoyances from crowding out issues of great magnitude. When we stop and look at the little things that annoy us, we soon see that they are of no consequence compared to the big things in life which should concern us. Especially in a day like this, when issues of great magnitude are at stake, to fret over little things is actually sinful. Perhaps all of us catch ourselves doing it and remember what is happening in the world, and then we are ashamed.

The little disturbances of daily living often mar our spirits until some tragic event stuns us, and then it is we see how foolish our worry was. A friend of mine lost her husband, which broke her heart. While we were talking about it, she said, "You know, the little things that used to worry me do not matter any more. That which used to disturb me doesn't bother me any more. I used to fret when he was a little late for meals and let his tardiness ruin my whole day. But now, he won't be coming home any more."

Life is so fleeting. The days of our years are so few. And Christmas helps us see life in proper proportion. It becomes for us a big event that overshadows the little annoyances of life. The petty concerns of our everyday living lose their importance in the light of the Christ.

And finally, Christmas is a time to keep the glitter of the material from crowding out God's revelation in Christ. If we would catch the real meaning of Christmas, our commercialization of it must give way to its spiritual significance. We should never get away from the fact that the reason we celebrate is because Jesus was born almost two thousand years ago, an event which has changed the course of history. It is a time to remember this.

AIDS TO WORSHIP

Hymns: "Joy to the World"
"O Little Town of Bethlehem"
Scripture: Luke 2:8-20

A Prayer

Dear God, simply but sincerely we lift our hearts to thee, saying, "Thank you for Jesus!" We remember the first announcement of his coming and the words that linger in our memories: "Fear not . . . good tidings . . . great joy . . . all people . . . Savior . . . Christ the Lord."

It is a long way from Bethlehem to our homes; it is a long way from a crib in a stable to a crib in our own hearts; it is a long time since that first Christmas to this Christmas; but as new life came into the world then, it is our faith that it can come into our lives today.

> We confess that—
> Though Christ a thousand times
> In Bethlehem be born,
> If He's not born in thee
> Thy soul is still forlorn.

Over the tumult of our world and the noise of the marketplace, may the voice of Christ ring clear and true, speaking the word of peace and reconciliation to our wayward ways. In his name we offer our prayer. Amen.

Index

141